WHAT PEOPLE ARE S

BELIEVE AND I1 1S TRUE

Authentic and moving. Deborah Lloyd shares a down to earth and intimate story that will inspire courage, trust, and help us remember that "miracles" are our human birthright. An unforgettable journey into the deeper, and often-overlooked, aspects of healing.

Llyn Roberts, M.A.

Author of *Shamanic Reiki* and *Shapeshifting into Higher Consciousness*

By sharing her own courageous experiences with spiritual and physical healing, Deborah Lloyd inspires us to take the next step on our journey. The message of this book is one that radiates hope and encouragement for anyone seeking a more profound relationship with inner peace.

Carole J. Obley,

Author of *I'm Still with You*

Every person who wants to open their lives more fully and embrace their spiritual life, should read this book! Spirituality, as described in Deborah's book, is the medicine for whatever ails you on the physical, mental and emotional levels. I highly recommend it to anyone who is on a spiritual path or anyone who desires to have a greater understanding of spiritual energy.

Nancy Mramor, Ph.D.

Award winning author of *Spiritual Fitness*

This beautiful autobiography is uplifting and empowering. Deb Lloyd writes the way she lives her life...from the heart, with honesty, compassion, and love.

Nancy Gordon, Ph.D.

Author of *A Guiding Philosophy for the Future of Healthcare: It's Not What You Think...Actually It Is What You Think!*

Believe
and it is True

A Story of Healing and Life Lessons

Believe
and it is True

A Story of Healing and Life Lessons

Deborah K. Lloyd

BOOKS

Winchester, UK
Washington, USA

First published by O-Books, 2012
O-Books is an imprint of John Hunt Publishing Ltd., Laurel House, Station Approach,
Alresford, Hants, SO24 9JH, UK
office1@o-books.net
www.o-books.com

For distributor details and how to order please visit the 'Ordering' section on our website.

Text copyright: Deborah K. Lloyd 2011

ISBN: 978 1 84694 855 8

A CIP catalogue record for this book is available from the British Library.

Design: Stuart Davies

Printed in the USA by Edwards Brothers Malloy

We operate a distinctive and ethical publishing philosophy in all
areas of our business, from our global network of authors to
production and worldwide distribution.

CONTENTS

BELIEVE AND IT IS TRUE!

This book is unique. I am writing about a healing, a miracle. Unlike other books, I am not describing a miracle that happened to me, in the past. Rather, I am writing about a miracle, a healing, that is occurring right now, and it is continuing to occur, over time. I am saying "yes" to many opportunities to learn lessons and to grow in my spiritual awareness and, somehow, I am finding the grace to embrace these opportunities. We are given many opportunities during our lifetimes to learn lessons, but often we ignore the inspirational thoughts that come into our minds.

I know I am being healed, but I am not certain what part, or parts, of me are being healed. Rather, I believe that the whole of me is being healed and that this healing will affect every aspect of my being – my body, my mind, and my soul. It started a long time ago, but I have only recently become aware of it. The healing process has undergone a transformation and it is now proceeding along with rapid speed. I am cooperating with it. No, in fact, I am making it happen. It is through my own will and intention that it is moving forward. The possibility of healing was always available to me. I just did not see it. I did not believe, for most of my life, that it was even possible. I thought miracles were rare events, happening to other people, people who are holy, in the religious sense of the word.

My story is uniquely my story and yet it is everyone's story. I share it with you to teach that anything is possible. When a person becomes aware of the powers of the Universe (God, the Source, Spirit – use whatever word is comfortable for you), and learns to access this power, awesome results can occur. These results can be beyond our wildest imaginings. Miracles and joyous events could replace all the problems of the world. If every human being believed in the possibility of manifesting only loving and healing energies, all the problems in the world would simply disappear. There would be no negative energies to feed them. All negative manifestations would be transformed into positive energies.

Back to my story...I am an ordinary woman who is living an extraordinary life. I know now, before my birth, I chose the circumstances of my life to bring me to this point of under-standing. I have moved from "believing" to "knowing." There is no doubt, throughout the tapestry of my being, that the Universe has great powers. I know the existence of an Universal Power that is far greater and spectacular than our human brains can conceive. I can tap into this Power simply by recognizing it exists all around me, and it exists within me. Throughout the ages, we have tried to describe it, quantify it, measure it, and teach it, to no avail. It is not possible to define something that is indefinable!! We simply have to recognize it and live within Its wisdom.

So now, let me tell you my story....

Deborah K. Lloyd

(The names of the healing practitioners in this book have been changed, as my memories and perceptions may not necessarily match the healers'!)

Chapter 1

THE EARLY YEARS

Mom was a storyteller, and there were certain stories that we three oldest girls heard over and over again, in our large farmhouse kitchen. Every night after supper, the four of us gathered around the old white enamel kitchen sink. Mom washed the dishes, placing them in the red drying rack, and we three girls dried them, while listening to another family tale. One of our favorite stories was the exciting courtship of Mom and Dad. She always told the romantic tale with a large smile on her pretty face.

Once upon a time, there was a young man who noticed a pretty young girl in his parish church. Both of them were Indiana farm kids, living only several miles apart. They had attended different schools as the township line separated their farms. And he was four years older than she, so he had already graduated from high school when she began her freshman year.

She had always admired him from afar, thinking he was a really cute guy, but he was popular, a high school basketball star, and he even had his own car. She was not popular at all and thought he did not even know her name. After his high school graduation, he farmed with his father and saved all his money to buy his own farm. When she graduated, she found a job in a local factory. One night, she and her sister were sitting on the front steps, talking and watching an occasional car drive by. They noticed that Jim Roy, the cute guy from church, drove by, and then he promptly turned around and pulled into their driveway! He walked over to her and her sister and asked my Mom out on a date. She could not believe that he was actually interested in her! They soon fell in love, he bought his farm, they got married and began their new life together.

The farm had a dilapidated house on it, so they lived with his parents for over a year. He was very busy, starting his own farm and repairing the old farmhouse. They also welcomed their first baby that summer, a pretty little girl who looked like her mother. They loved their little girl, Debbie. Although his parents already had a number of grandchildren, his father took a special liking to his newest little granddaughter and spent many hot summer evenings, walking her around the parlor, soothing her fussiness. By the time the young couple was ready to move into their own home, their second child was on the way. They welcomed their second daughter that summer. Life was busy and full of joy.

The summer of 1956 brought more joy, as their third daughter joined the family. But the fall brought great sadness. It seemed the polio epidemic was finally coming to an end, although it had not totally vanished. In fact, their little girls had already received the first two vaccination doses, and they thought the fear of polio striking their children was behind them.

Then, one morning, three-year-old Debbie walked up to the kitchen table for breakfast, and her legs collapsed beneath her. She simply fell to the floor. She looked bewildered and stood up again, only to fall again. Mom called Dad in from the barn, and he tried to reassure her that it probably was nothing to be concerned about, although he himself was very worried. They dropped the other girls off at his parents, and rushed Debbie to the family doctor. By now, she could not stand at all. While it was unusual that she did not have the typical flu-like symptoms of polio, the doctor told them there was nothing else it could be. It had to be polio. They brought her home and waited anxiously for the next days, and weeks, to see how she would do.

During her storytelling, Mom minimized the devastation she must have felt watching Debbie (me) trying to walk during those first few weeks. She would continue the tale…. They found some relief in the fact that only Debbie's legs were affected; and that neither her lungs, nor any other part of her body, were damaged. Eventually, she was able to move her legs a little and could stand with their help. Within a few months, she was fitted with metal braces and wooden crutches, and could walk again. It was a sad situation, but life goes on, and everyone made the best of it.

A second tragedy struck Mom and Dad, only seven months later, when Dad's father suffered a major heart attack and died immediately. Dad, being the youngest son, had always been close to his father – and although Grandpa had been greatly saddened by my polio, he had been an anchor to Dad during those difficult days.

The loving marriage continued, and the babies kept coming. Dad was very happy when the next two babies were boys, as he finally had two sons, very important on a farm. Then the difficult summer of 1960 happened. The family doctor told Mom and Dad about a young orthopedic surgeon who had started a practice in Fort Wayne. He thought it was worth a try to take me to see him, perhaps something could be done for me. The doctor was performing a new surgical technique; this technique involved transferring ligaments and muscles from the legs to rebuild the feet. Two operations were scheduled for that summer – one in June for my right leg and feet, and another in July for the left. And Mom was expecting baby number six in June.

As it turned out, Mom gave birth to a baby girl, Patty, in the same hospital the day before my first operation was scheduled. She was on one floor in the hospital, and I was on another. As soon as Mom was discharged from the hospital, she dropped the baby off with a grandmother, along with the other four children, and sat with me in the hospital room, hour after hour after hour. On the tenth day, I was released from the hospital and the entire family was reunited again.

What a long, hot summer that was. Since I was fitted with full leg casts and not allowed to put any weight on my legs, I was confined to sitting on the couch during the day. I became the official babysitter, holding and playing with the new baby, Patty. What fun that was for a little seven-year-old girl! It was like having a living baby doll, one who could smile back and coo with you. This became the happiest part of my recuperation.

One night, Patty became ill, and Mom and Dad rushed her to the hospital. I remember their sad faces the following morning when they told us she had died at the hospital during the night. They could barely cope with yet another tragedy, but they did what they had to do. I remember Dad carrying me, with casts on my legs, and a pretty pink dress, to her little casket, with tears running down his face – the only time I remember him crying. I remember her quiet little body in the casket and saying good-bye to her. Mom often talked about finding some comfort in believing she had a little angel in heaven, but there was always a tinge of sadness in this comfort.

Life went on, and our family was blessed with four more children. With nine children, there were many good times, and many hard times. Life was busy on a farm, raising beef cattle, growing a garden and canning, working the fields. We were bright kids, good students, well-behaved. We had many fun times and enjoyed playing games and cards. Money was scarce, and we children had wants that could not be granted. My biggest desire was to take piano lessons, but my parents could not afford it.

At the same time, we counted the blessings that we had. Dad often said we ate better than most people, with our large freezer filled with beef, and a cupboard stocked with canned, garden-grown vegetables. I grew up with the idea that we just needed to make the best of what we had. Maybe we could not afford to take a vacation, but we could have lots of fun at home.

Then, in 1971 the really big tragedy hit our household. Dad was diagnosed with leukemia, and five months later, he joined our baby sister in heaven. Mom could barely cope with every-thing – her overwhelming grief that no one seemed to understand, or wanted to hear about; nine young children with all their childhood needs, as well as a large farm to contend with.

The story lost its magic, and the storytelling ended.

Lesson #1: Everyone has a story, full of learning opportunities.

CHAPTER 2

THE GIFT OF FAITH

Throughout the ages, believing in a Divine God has often been relegated to the organized religions. Unfortunately our religions have attempted to define a Presence that is beyond the words of a definition. Words are finite, and God is the Infinite Being. And, yet, many of our faith journeys begin with religious practice, and continue to be enriched with religious practice – including my own.

Catholic religion was a part of our life on the farm. We attended Mass every Sunday and did not work on Sundays, often spending our afternoons visiting grandparents and other relatives. Practicing my Catholic religion has always been a very important part of my life. I have fond memories of meaningful life events – my First Communion Day, our wedding Mass, the baptisms of our children. I love to visit old churches and sit in the quiet respite from my busy and noisy life. I cherish magnificent religious art that can be found in the most humble of church buildings. Some religious music touches my heart in a way that no other music can.

While I honor my religion, some teachings of the Catholic Church have always presented a challenge to me. And, more importantly, some actions of the Church seem in total opposition to the Truth, especially in recent scandals. Equality of the sexes, unfortunately, is not a value of the Church, but it certainly is a strong value to me. The hierarchal structure and rules and regulations can stifle the worth of each human being, male and female. The Church holds many Truths but historically, at certain times, the Church leaders, human men with egos, have buried these Truths under man-made laws that have diminished, or hidden, Truth.

I have never been convinced that the Catholic Church, or any other Christian, or non-Christian, denomination, is the end-all and be-all of all Truth. I love to read about other religious traditions and spiritual beliefs, and I have found beautiful Truths living in the teachings of other religions and cultures. At the same time, there is an underlying thread throughout all these religious teachings. There are more similarities than differences, but many Church leaders of diverse faith traditions contend their beliefs are the only right ones. It's puzzling. Although I still cherish my Catholic upbringing, the groundwork to explore other possibilities has always been a part of my life. My mind and heart have always been open to the possibility of finding other truths, in other ways.

I have always been an introspective and deep-thinking person, and spending most of my childhood sitting around, while my siblings were outside playing, gave me many opportunities to think about my life, my faith, and finding meaning in my circumstances. My family was a practicing Catholic family and all of us children attended Catholic grade school. Not attending Sunday Mass was unthinkable – you had to be a very sick child to be excused! We believed in heaven and hell, and purgatory and limbo. We believed in the saints and participated in the Sacraments. We learned about guardian angels, and my guardian angel was my best friend on those long, lonely afternoons on the couch.

I often wondered why God chose me to have polio, and not my brothers and sisters, or my parents, or any of my other relatives. One day, while still quite young, about six or seven years old, I remember finding a solution to that problem. I imagined a scenario where God gave me the choice. He asked me, "Do you want to have polio, or do you want your children to have it?" That was an easy question. Without any hesitation, I told God I would accept the illness willingly, rather than giving it to my future children. It was painful to see strangers stare at me in a store, or classmates look at my legs. It was painful not to have the ability to play like other children. Never, never, ever, would I want my future children to experience that kind of pain and sadness. I carried that imaginary scenario in my heart throughout my entire childhood. It gave me solace and comfort. I saw God as a Being of love and goodness to me, and my faith carried me through many dark hours.

My faith provided the explanation for all the blessings I received in my adult years, too. As a teenager, I'd spent many nights crying myself to sleep over not having dates in high school and believing that no guy would ever love me, with my atrophied legs and severe limp. I had prayed many, many times for a good, loving man who would accept me and love me, just the way I was. Being an "old maid" was simply not an acceptable option to me. The ideal life included a happy marriage and having a family. I wanted the kind of love I saw between my parents, and I wanted to be a mother one day.

About six weeks after my Dad's death, I met my husband – I was all of 18 years old, and Gary was just 20 years old. Gary was the answer to all my prayers, being a very kind and gentle man. He saw beyond the polio and my physical limitations. We immediately felt like old soul mates who felt a very strong connection and loved each other deeply. My prayers were answered!

Our wedding day was magnificent, although it was a cold, wintry day in Indiana. Immediately after we said our vows, in the little Catholic Church of my childhood, the sun came out from behind the clouds and shone through the stained glass windows, casting a beautiful light throughout the church. Many guests told us the sunlight lit up my dress with a heavenly glow, and it was a memorable experience for them. I always saw that special light as a sign of God's blessings and Dad's approval on our marriage. Our Catholic faith became the foundation for our marriage.

I felt very blessed to have lived through a difficult childhood and living a fulfilling adulthood, with a good, loving husband. It seemed I could define my life in two parts, the early difficult years, and then the fun, blessed years of marriage. It seemed all the prayers of my childhood had been answered. Even though I did not use the term, Gift of Faith, for most of my life, I lived it fully. My faith was the foundation of my beliefs and the basis of how I lived my life.

Faith is simply a a belief in a Higher Power. It seems people in every tradition and culture have a belief in a Higher Power, whether they call it God, Yahweh, Great Spirit, Source, Universe, the list goes on. And, it seems every person innately knows that some actions are simply right, and some things are always wrong. For example, people of all cultures and religions know that to kill another person, for no valid reason, is always wrong. ("Valid" reasons may include a just war, protection of a human life, or protection of one's property.) The words to articulate each of these beliefs vary from culture to culture, religion to religion. These beliefs are instilled in each person's heart, and it is not necessary, although it can be helpful, to participate in any particular religion to know these truths. Each person can simply listen, with honesty and openness, to the stirrings of Spirit within his or her own heart.

Sometimes we do not listen to our hearts at all and do things that are totally against Spirit, the Spirit within ourselves and within others. Or we hear the voices of our hearts and ignore them because our fear, greed, or self-centeredness has become the ruling guide in our lives. We are living outside universal truths, and a lack of balance between our minds, bodies and spirits becomes a way of life. When we decide to act against truth, there will be negative consequences, sooner or later, in this lifetime, or the next.

The underlying basis of all universal truths is love – love of our Supreme Being, ourselves, others, and nature. There is a true harmony and peacefulness that cannot be achieved in any other way.

Like many people, I often lived these truths, as a result of my religious upbringing and practice, and the moral integrity that defines my life. However, a deeper understanding grew when I made the conscientious decision to explore these truths more fully. In some cases, I only became aware of the impact of some of these truths in recent years. These truths have enabled my story of healing to occur, as I became more aware and lived them more fully – although being human, I frequently veered off track.

The greatest gift of my lifetime is faith – pure and simple. When faith is fully expressed, it moves from a belief, to a knowing. Doubt disappears. Belief is the acknowledgement that something exists out there, an intellectual exercise. Knowing is a deep knowledge of the heart, living within the soul. It is the recognition of the Universal Force, God, a Supreme Being, a Divine Source, Spirit. If this basic awareness is not present, the other gifts from God may not be recognized.

Simply put, the Gift of Faith is truly a blessing!

Lesson #2: Faith in God is a true blessing.

CHAPTER 3

LEARNING LIFE LESSONS

Our lives are like roller coasters, with many up's and down's and unexpected curves in-between. We can even hang upside down for awhile! We can derail, or fly at lightning speed, in the wrong direction, and eventually wreck. Then, we pick ourselves up and carry our cars back to the rails, and ride on the right track again. Life can be quite an adventure.

Although I am relating my story through being a student of recent life lessons, I am aware that lessons were being given to me all along. They were operational during all the times of my life. My lack of awareness did not stop the power of the lessons. However, my lack of awareness resulted in my not realizing, or living, the full potentiality of them. It is like having the Book of All Truths on a bookshelf in your home, and you never take the time to open the book and read it. The Book was there all along, but the benefits were negligible since you did not make the effort to learn about them.

My life seemed to be going along just fine - until my physical condition started to change in the early 1990s. My normal, suburban life had been serene during our first seventeen years of marriage. Gary's career as a mechanical engineer took us to Cincinnati, Ohio; Providence, Rhode Island; and Pittsburgh, Pennsylvania. We had two children, a son and a daughter. The pregnancies were uneventful, a pleasant surprise to the doctors, and to us. The doctors did not know if my weakened hips and legs would be able to carry the extra weight during pregnancy, or if I would be on bed rest for the last few months. No problems at all, I was physically active until the births took place. We were told that while my legs were weak, my strong stomach and back muscles enabled me to carry the babies throughout the full nine months. We knew God had blessed us tremendously.

While raising the children, I was a stay-at-home mother, but a very busy one. Gary and I did a great deal of volunteer work in our Catholic parish community, becoming involved with the Marriage Encounter and engaged couples programs. When our children were in elementary school, I was ready to embark on a career where I could help other people. I fulfilled a secret wish by attending college and obtained Bachelor's and Master's degrees in the field of social work. I knew what it was like to live through difficulties and still have a good life. I knew if I could help others to do the same, it would be meaningful work.

My work as a social worker in a children's hospital involved walking up and down long hospital corridors, between the nurses' station and patients' rooms, all day long. The evenings at home were busy preparing dinner, doing household chores, and sharing in the driving trips, taking our children to various practices and activities.

A fatigue came over me that was unusual and frightening. My entire body felt heavy and tired, and sometimes it took more effort than I had simply to walk across a room. It felt like I was trying to walk through mud, slugging along, and wondering if I'd ever reach the other side. I learned what the phrase, "hitting the wall," really meant.

Some days, when I walked through the front door after a long day at work, nothing sounded better than going to bed, and not having to move my body at all. But, I would not permit myself to do that. I wanted to be the perfect wife and mother, and live the life I had always dreamed. After a few months of living with this increasing fatigue, my knees and legs started to hurt. This was a new phenomenon to me, as the only physical pain I'd ever experienced from the polio was pain resulting after the surgeries in 1960. Pain had never been a part of my life, but now it seemed my entire body was changing – and not for the better. It was terrifying.

One day, I saw a newspaper article describing a new occurrence for people who'd had polio, called Post-Polio Syndrome. It seemed many polio survivors were experiencing many of the same things I was, and many of them were experiencing even more severe symptoms. Polio survivors who had been affected in their lungs and throats were having new problems with breathing and swallowing. Polio survivors who had been affected in their limbs, like me, were losing muscle strength and becoming weaker. The article stated some polio survivors even lost all physical functioning of those limbs. There was even conjecture that the polio virus could be re-attacking the same people again.

Few doctors in Pittsburgh seemed to be aware of this new phenomenon, and through my library research (these were the days before the Internet), I found three places in the country where post-polio patients were being evaluated and treated. The closest one was at the University of Michigan in Ann Arbor, so I made an appointment and the four of us took a long weekend trip to its clinic.

To say the least, it was a jarring experience to hear the compassionate doctor, with tears in his eyes, confirm that I had all the symptoms of Post-Polio Syndrome. His explanation was that polio victims had lost muscle mass and strength when polio struck. As healthy people age, muscle strength is lost, but they are losing it from a starting place of 100% physical functioning. Polio victims, on the other hand, lose muscle strength from a lower level of functioning, perhaps as low as 50% of normal functioning. So the inevitable losses seemed to have a much larger impact.

Also, he explained, muscles and ligaments were relocated in the body during the surgeries of the 1960s. These muscles are simply wearing out, as they were transferred to parts of the body where they were not meant to be used. The operations that I had were exactly that procedure – muscles and ligaments were moved from less-affected parts of my legs, to build up my very weak feet.

He stated the right leg pain was a result of knee misalignment. There was a bony "knob" on the inside of my right knee, indicating the joint was not aligned properly. His recommendations included a leg brace, use of a cane, and energy conservation. He gave me strong instructions to walk less and, when I started to feel tired, to simply stop all activities for the day. He said the best scenario that I could hope for was to maintain what abilities I had right then, and not to lose any more physical strength. He explained there was no way to ever regain the strength back when lost - no surgeries, no medications, no exercise, nothing. And, he confirmed, some post-polio survivors are losing everything, re-experiencing paralysis and sadly having to use wheelchairs. He recommended that I should do everything in my power to keep the physical abilities I currently had.

I was devastated by this news, but would not allow myself to wallow in despair. A new fear started to grow in my mind - that I could lose all physical ability to walk and spend the rest of my life in a wheelchair. I was determined that would never happen to me.

My old steel-like determination was back! I would slow down and allow my family to do more around the house and for me. I reverted back to my childhood days, when my goals were to be the perfect patient, the perfect little girl who kept a smile on her face, even when she was sad and lonely inside. I would be the perfect, best post-polio survivor ever! And being a survivor was the goal. I had always had strong feelings about not living my life as a victim, and I was determined to maintain that mentality. I would keep my active and fulfilling life as normal as possible.

My prayer life went into high gear. I prayed, I pleaded, I begged. I asked God to please, please, please, not let me end up with total paralysis again. I did not want to spend the rest of my life in a wheelchair. I did not want to be a victim. I saw one ray of sunlight in the wheelchair scenario, however. At least, I had a career where I could work in a wheelchair. In fact, I decided to leave my job as a hospital social worker and return to my earlier work as a psychotherapist. Sitting in a chair, in a therapy room with clients, would be easier on my legs, and besides, I truly enjoyed working with people in therapy. Changing my career path reiterated my commitment to maintaining a meaningful life, while responding to new physical considerations.

In those days, I was setting up an expectation, and your life is exactly what you picture. We often hear phrases like, "self-fulfilling prophecy," or "you get what you ask for." Expectations can work for you, or against you. Many of us think "inside the box" so our expectations stay within that box. We do not expect anything spectacular, or miraculous. We set limits on our lives, limits that could be expanded, if we gave it any thought or attention. We set up expectations, and then we live our whole lives in these small, defined boxes.

My goal, my expectation, was to maintain my current physical condition, and that is exactly what happened. I maintained the same level of functionality, and that seemed really good to me. Compared to other polio survivors, it seemed I was successfully beating the effects of the disease, for the second time around.

Living within these expectations, though, resulted in some not-so-positive realities in my life. I was living within a reinforcement of my old, unspoken beliefs. I took the doctor's words to heart. I focused on what I could not do, rather than what I could do. Many times, I felt like the little girl lying on the couch, pretending to feel happy and acting as if everything was normal.

However, there were also some positive effects for me. The doctor had complimented me on keeping my weight within the normal range for my height. Being overweight is a common problem for polio victims, as physical activity can be limited. So, I was more committed than ever to eating healthily, keeping my weight in a good range, and maintaining my already-limited physical abilities.

The next ten years were full of fun and busy events, as our children grew up, attended excellent colleges, and began their careers. My career also expanded into a new phase of supervisory and management positions. Gary and I loved our freedom, enjoying evenings with friends, dinners at nice restaurants, the theater, and travel. My fatigue was kept at bay, as there was less physical activity needed to maintain a home for two empty-nesters.

My expectation was to maintain my current physical status. The possibility of improvement was not on my radar screen. And I received exactly what I expected – I maintained my physical strength and got along fine. I began to feel more confident that I would obtain the best goal that the doctor had established for me - maintaining the physical strength that I still had. And, I was pleased that I was reaching that goal.

Lesson #3: We create our reality through our expectations.

CHAPTER 4

STEPPING BEYOND EXPECTATIONS

God's plan for us is often greater than we can imagine. He will invite us to something better, dropping hints here and there. We can stay in our comfort zone and ignore these invitations, or we can pursue them, and find great growth and blessings. God gave me such an opportunity.

I had always believed that God places people in our lives to help us along our paths, just at the right time. We then have the choice to say "yes" to the invitation, or to say "no" by ignoring that person or the message she brings.

It was a typical day at the office. Because I was the manager of our growing mental health clinic, I had the task of interviewing psychotherapists for a new position. During one interview, the candidate mentioned she'd just become a Reiki Master and hoped to integrate it into her work in our clinic, if she was offered the position. I had no idea what being a Reiki Master meant. I responded in a very unusual way when the applicant mentioned something in an interview that I did not understand – I did not ask a follow-up question! Because she had the kind of experience our clinic needed, she was offered the position and she accepted it. During her first day on the job, I asked more about the technique she had mentioned during the interview.

She explained Reiki is an ancient Japanese form of energy healing. I had never heard the term, "energy healing" before this moment. She described how she could lay her hands on a person, and Universal Life Force energy came through her hands and went to the area where a person required healing. Because this energy could be relaxing to a client, the energy could unblock a resistance to discuss difficult topics. It could open doors for growth during therapy sessions.

Being the responsible manager that I try to be, I replied that I'd need to check with the administrators of this Catholic agency. I would also need to check with the insurance companies, to make sure she could use this method during her therapy sessions with her clients. Surprisingly, the Executive Director of the agency had heard of Reiki and had no problem with her using it. The insurance companies viewed it as another form of relaxation, not unlike breathing exercises or visualization techniques that many therapists use as an adjunct to talk therapy, so there were no problems with the companies either. She got the go-ahead to use Reiki.

My emotional reaction was one of great skepticism. It sounded "off-the-wall" to me, too non-traditional, and I wondered if we really should be allowing its use at our agency. I had never heard of energy healing, and the idea that someone could lay hands on another person, and healing energies would come through them, sounded almost sacrilegious. There were Bible stories of Jesus laying hands on people, and to think a psychotherapist in Pittsburgh could do the same thing seemed rather outlandish. However, I also had high regards for this psychotherapist's professional expertise and decided I'd keep an open mind. What if it really worked? Breaking through clients' resistances can be a difficult task, and anything was certainly worth a try.

As the weeks passed, this therapist shared stories with our staff about her therapeutic successes, by using Reiki at the beginning of her sessions. It seemed her clients became relaxed very quickly, and they shared more freely. It seemed her clients progressed more rapidly than those who only experienced talk therapy. It was really eye-opening to the rest of us, and we began to think about the possibility of more of our therapists becoming trained in the technique.

This therapist also talked to me privately about the possibility of Reiki helping my legs and my energy level, and she offered to work with me. Her offer was not comfortable for me, as I knew in a relaxed state I may share more than what would be appropriate to share with someone who reported to me. I knew my polio experience and my post-polio challenges were still highly-charged emotional areas for me. I did not want to cry, or express whatever emotions that may lie within me, with an employee.

I wanted to give Reiki a try, though, so I asked about seeing the person who had trained her. I was very surprised to learn that she had been trained by a Catholic nun - obviously, a progressive one. That fact gave me considerable comfort, in trying to reconcile my Catholic beliefs with this new-to-me energy-healing technique. I stirred up the courage to make an appointment for a Reiki session.

What do you do? What do you say? What do you wear? My head was filled with many questions, and my body was filled with great anxiety. I felt like I was going on a great adventure, but I had no information or details about it. I did not know what to expect. And, yet, it felt like it was something I simply had to do - something, or Someone, was pulling me in that direction.

Within a few minutes, calmness overcame me as the kind and gentle Sister instructed me to lie on the massage table and relax. My first Reiki session was an absolute delight! Not only did I feel more relaxed, but I also felt the tiredness from the daily busyness of my life lift out of my body. The aches and pains in my legs decreased during the session. I scheduled another session for the following week.

Gary also became intrigued and decided to experience a Reiki session, too. The nun also provided Reiki trainings and suggested that we could access Reiki on a regular basis by both of us attending the class and giving Reiki to each other frequently. In the long run, it could save us lots of money. We decided to do it.

Gary's main purpose in learning Reiki was to help me. He'd

always wanted to be able to do more for me, but it seemed there was nothing he could do, except to help more with the physical activities around the house. Reiki could be a whole new avenue of giving me actual physical support.

My decision to learn Reiki involved both my professional life and my personal life. It seemed it would be advantageous for me to have a better understanding of a new method being utilized with our clients. And, I certainly was excited that Reiki may help me in minimizing the post-polio symptoms.

The weekend was meaningful to both of us. We loved learning and using Reiki. It gradually became a significant part of our lives. Gary started to give me full-body treatments, lasting about an hour. I also gave myself brief treatments before falling asleep and upon awakening most mornings, probably about 10-15 minutes each time. As the weeks went by, Reiki became a daily practice. My fatigue level decreased dramatically, and the aches in my legs were less frequent and less severe. The energy level within my body continued to rise. It was wonderful to come home from work and feel like cooking and working around the house again.

About six weeks after our training, on a hot summer evening, I was reading in our sunroom. I lifted my eyes from the page and looked down at my legs, resting on an ottoman. I could not believe my eyes. Could it be true? Have my legs changed? I moved my right leg, back and forth, looking at it from all angles. Remember the bony knob that had been on my right knee, the knob noted by the post-polio doctor in Michigan? The knob that had indicated the joint misalignment and caused frequent pain? The knob was no longer there, it was gone. I called Gary into the sunroom, and he concurred – my knee had changed. It was now aligned properly, looking like my left knee. We were beyond astonished, and we simply stared at each other, in total disbelief. Neither the pain nor the knob has ever returned, to this day.

This was my first physical-healing miracle, a result of the

healing energies of Reiki practice. I continued to thank God for this amazing, miraculous gift over and over. It was so exciting to see a concrete result. I was becoming less tired and more energized. It was a concrete sign that Reiki was working for me.

Five months later, Gary and I attended Reiki II training. Each level of training enables the practitioner to access a stronger level of energy healing. Also, during Reiki II, we learned how to do "distance healing," which means sending Reiki to anyone, or any situation, in the world. All one needs to do is to set the intention and hold one's hands outward. This practice was comfortable to me, as I viewed it as a type of prayer. Just as I can pray for anything or anyone in the world, I can send the powerful, healing energies of Reiki to anyone anywhere.

I've read, in several places, that the use of Reiki can be instrumental in raising one's level of consciousness and opening one's heart and mind to new possibilities. In our Reiki trainings, the chakra system was introduced to us. This system is part of an Indian tradition and is also taught in yoga classes. Chakras are energy centers in our bodies, and each chakra is associated with physical, emotional, and spiritual energy fields. Reiki is sent to the centers where healing is most needed.

I started to read many books about healthy lifestyles, alternative ways of healing, and spiritual traditions found in other cultures. New people seemed to show up in my life, each one adding a new perspective to my traditional beliefs. I opened myself to new possibilities in my own life. Reiki awakened parts of my Spirit that had been dormant most of my life.

I was learning a very important life lesson during this period. This lesson is paying attention to the opportunities God gives me, and saying "yes" to the opportunities. It would have been so easy to reject the possibility of Reiki in my life. It was different from anything I had ever experienced, and it seemed a little wacky, in the beginning. I had paid attention to this gift. I learned more about it, and I found the courage to make that first appointment.

First, I had paid attention to what the newly hired psychotherapist was using in her practice and explored the possibility of using Reiki in my own life. I had listened to those little nagging thoughts that I should schedule a Reiki session, and that I should learn how to do Reiki myself. Although my original focus in using Reiki was to ease physical problems, my focus soon expanded to include other aspects, such as obtaining new knowledge and facilitating further spiritual growth, beyond my upbringing as a traditional Catholic.

More importantly, I was focusing my attention on becoming physically stronger and healthier, rather than living in the fear of paralysis and being confined to a wheelchair for the remainder of my life. My focus had shifted 180 degrees. I began to visualize myself as walking around confidently, on my own two legs, even when I became elderly. Due to the recent changes, it had now become a viable possibility for me. My attention was focused on the fact that I could become healthier – physically and spiritually.

I was beginning on a new path of healthiness, growth and healing, one step at a time.

Lesson #4: When we say "yes" to God-given opportunities, wonderful things happen.

CHAPTER 5

RESISTANCE, TOO

Oh, my path has not been straightforward and smooth. It has been filled with many bumps and detours along the way. So many times, my head was filled with doubts and lack of belief. My journey has always been two steps forward and one backward. In my small Indiana town, I was often referred to as the "little girl with polio." And that became how I defined myself within the core of my being. In my mind, I stood out in the crowd for all the wrong reasons. So many areas of my life had been affected by this terrible childhood disease and it would be a long, slow process to change it all.

So many times, I saw myself as being defective and unworthy of the good things in life. Often, I did not see any possibility of becoming healthier or stronger. I had constructed unconscious roadblocks in my mind. I had put up barriers to living in full harmony with the Universe and lived a life of resistance to healing possibilities. What I did not understand, for most of my life, is that my thoughts and beliefs were creating my life, whether these thoughts and beliefs were positive and beneficial, or negative and self-defeating.

These negative thoughts create the "yes, buts" that all of us use in our day-to-day lives. Yes, I would like to work in a more peaceful environment, but I can't leave this job because it's secure, or no one else would pay me this salary, or fill in your own excuse. Yes, I'd like to eat healthier, but I don't have time to cook fresh foods. Yes, I'd like to get more exercise, but there is no good place to walk around here and who wants to drive to a park to walk? We become masters of great excuses! We are giving our own minds mixed messages, and then we send these mixed messages to the Universe – through our thoughts, actions and words. Then, we wonder why our lives seem so confusing, or unhappy, or disappointing. We have built up a strong wall of resistance to God's abundant blessings.

The world of God's unlimited possibilities is a world outside our limited belief systems and thought structures. Our thoughts and beliefs frequently prevent us from enjoying the great, overflowing abundances available to all of us. I lived with this resistance almost all my life, and it got a boost when I was diagnosed with Post-Polio Syndrome. Although I was experiencing less fatigue and less pain, I held onto too many old beliefs about my physical limitations.

One strong belief I'd developed during my childhood was that swimming was the only physical exercise available to me. As many physical activities involve running or strong stamina, this belief was not without some basis in reality. However, I did not put any time or energy into exploring other possibilities, as I did not think I would be able to do anything else. I never, ever, thought I'd have the physical strength and flexibility to do yoga, or any similar activity. Nor did I have any desire to humiliate myself in a class of physically agile and beautiful women that I imagined would attend a yoga class.

A friend had been trying to convince me, for several months, that I could do yoga and should accompany her to a class, but I always made an excuse not to join her. Finally, she invited Gary and me to join her and her husband in a special yoga event. (I think she realized the only way I might agree is to include Gary, my main support). This event combined yoga, chakra balancing and crystal bowl meditation. She reassured me the event was open to anyone, and that we did not have to be experienced in yoga to benefit from it. It was on a Friday evening, so I thought if I embarrassed myself, I'd have the rest of the weekend before I had to see her at work on Monday morning! The other reassuring part was the room would be darkened, and no one would see me very well. We could find the most far-off corner of the room for the class. The part of me that still felt embarrassed by my physical looks and atrophied legs was alive and well.

What do you do? What do you say? What do you wear? My head was filled with many questions, and my body was filled with great anxiety. I felt like I was going on a great adventure, but I had no information or details about it. I did not know what to expect. And, yet, it felt like it was something I simply had to do - something, or Someone, was pulling me in that direction.

It was really hard to say "yes" and attend that event, but I did. I could not believe how many poses I could actually do! I had not accounted for the fact that I have very strong core strength, having used my stomach muscles my whole life to assist me in walking. Some of the poses were quite easy for me, while others were difficult or nearly impossible for me to do. Because everyone was focused on their own poses and the room was relatively dark, it seemed no one even noticed what I could, or could not, do. I have to admit, at times, I looked at the other participants and realized others could not do some of the poses very well either. I let my fears and inhibitions go and truly enjoyed the class. It was an evening that changed my old belief that I was very limited in my ability to do physical activities.

In fact, Gary and I really enjoyed the evening and could not wait to participate in more yoga classes and events. I began to believe that yoga practice was something I could, and should, do. Most physical activities and sports were outside my comfort zone, or impossible to do, so it was a new experience for me to feel positive about any physical activity. Yoga became, and continues to be, an important part of my personal growth.

While yoga has its physical aspects, yoga also blends emotional and spiritual energies within the practice. Classes begin and end with meditation. All poses can be approached with a sense of openness and gratitude. I opened my body, and my heart, to this ancient tradition. I started to feel appreciation for my body and my spirit.

A common yoga phrase is "to be in your body." That was a new sensation for me – to connect my mind and spirit with my body, rather than live almost exclusively in my mind and spirit, and ignore my perceived unattractive body. I did not realize how disconnected I had become from my body. My old perception was that my body was defective, and it was the most unbecoming, and unattractive, aspect of my being.

There were yoga movements when I actually felt graceful, such as lifting my arms in a slow-moving arch, not unlike a lovely ballerina. Me – moving gracefully? That was the first time I ever remembered having such a preposterous thought. There were poses when I stood on one leg, while using the wall for support. Me – standing on one leg? An absolute impossibility in my mind, for the past fifty years of my life. New thoughts came to me, and I actually felt gratitude for my legs and feet having carried me, to the best of their ability, for the past fifty years. Me – being thankful for these too-skinny legs and very small feet, legs and feet that are marred by long surgical scars? That thought was a big, BIG first. I had spent over half a century living in negativity and fear, by not accepting and being thankful for my own physical body!

One evening, while driving home from a yoga class, I received an inspirational thought. It was simply "your body is beautiful." The last thing I had ever felt about my body was that it was beautiful – I could say I have a pretty face, or a nice dress, but I had never viewed myself as beautiful. People have always complimented me on my pretty smile. While it was a lovely compliment, I had also interpreted it in a negative manner – my smile was the one thing about me that was beautiful. In other words, my smile was lovely, and the rest of me was ugly. This one inspirational thought – my body is beautiful – stayed with me for days and brought great healing to my emotional self.

I started to leave behind my old beliefs, and to grow beyond this wall of resistance. I was reconnecting to my beautiful physical body, and that new belief opened up a whole new world of possibilities. While running a marathon may not be in my future, simply being a participant in yoga was earth-shattering to me. Practicing yoga became another miracle in my life journey. Bursting through these barriers that were built in my own mind was an important step towards future miracles.

Yoga began a universal flow of positive thoughts and energies to my physical body, while healing my emotional being and strengthening my spiritual self. The Universe is full of abundance and has many gifts available to us. We only have to quit resisting these gifts and accept them with open arms and genuine gratitude. It is true – the more gifts we accept from the Universe, the more we receive. So simple, and yet so profound.

Lesson #5: The Universe graces us with many gifts, when we are open to receiving them.

CHAPTER 6

ANOTHER CONNECTION

John Edward, a medium who has a national television show, was becoming more well-known. I watched him from time to time, and often wondered if my parents could communicate with me, from the other side. I continued to cherish memories of my father, although his death had occurred a few decades earlier. My mother had recently died, and I wondered if she was watching all nine of her adult children, and her many grandchildren.

I had grown up with traditional beliefs about heaven, but these beliefs had not included the possibility of communication with our deceased parents, relatives, and other ancestors. In Catholic school, we'd been taught that we could pray to the saints requesting their intercession with God, talking to Him on our behalf. But, as far as I knew, only God, or the angels delivering His messages, could communicate with us while we lived on earth. And those occasions were rare and seemed to be reserved for special people. I believed you had to be a saint to be so blessed with this kind of direct communication.

While Pittsburgh is not exactly a hotbed of liberal thinking, there are small groups of people who think in alternative ways. One of my friends was attending programs at a local new-age-type bookstore, and she shared the contents of these programs with me. A local psychic medium, Valerie, was doing a gallery event (similar to a John Edward TV show), and I decided to attend. Part of me was excited – and part of me was anxious.

What do you do? What do you say? What do you wear? My head was filled with many questions, and my body was filled with great anxiety. I felt like I was going on a great adventure, but I had no infor-mation or details about it. I did not know what to expect. And, yet, it felt like it was something I simply had to do - something, or Someone, was pulling me in that direction.

This time, my new adventure felt "safer." I imagined myself slipping into a large conference room, and sliding into a seat in the back row. Perhaps no one would notice me. I doubted anyone in the room would know me, as most of our friends would probably not attend such an event.

Three rows of chairs were placed in a semi-circle in a small, comfortable room. Approximately fifteen people were in attendance, and I was able to find a chair at the end of the second row, not too obvious. Valerie began the evening by explaining how she receives her information. She sees and hears the spirits of the deceased and relays the information they give to her.

I was stunned by some of the readings Valerie gave. Her information was specific and detailed. A reading that I will never forget was one she gave to a couple who sat directly in front of me. It was obvious from the beginning that the husband was uncomfortable and wishing he had not come, as he shifted in his chair and looked down at the floor. When Valerie walked over to them, she stated a young teenage boy was there and asked if they knew who he was. The wife stated he was their son, who had died a few months earlier. Through Valerie, the son told his parents he was fine and was with them often, and he gave several examples of his presence. He related seeing his mother giving his black leather jacket and his cherished CD's to his younger brother. He referred to several recent incidents in the family that were humorous. While both parents sobbed, and laughed, during the reading, both expressed finding great comfort in the knowledge their son continued to live in spirit, and continued to be a part of their family life.

The medium spent the last minutes of the program answering questions from the audience. I was somewhat disappointed that neither of my parents had come through for me. But I was finally able to ask a question. I have a reoccurring phenomenon and wondered what the significance could be. I often find shiny pennies, especially when I am upset, or going through some kind of difficulty. I asked if there was significance in my finding shiny pennies often. Valerie replied yes, the pennies are a gift from one of my great-grandmothers, letting me know that she is around me and supporting me throughout my life. She described this great-grandmother's appearance. I have pictures of all four of my great-grandmothers and know which one is the giver of the pennies.

Then Valerie said, "Your mother is now standing behind you." Mom showed Valerie a scene with Mom and me in a cemetery. I was writing information from tombstones on a little notepad, as Mom was giving me information about the relatives. I was amazed, as Valerie described the scene, exactly as it had happened. Before her illnesses, Mom and I had visited several local cemeteries to obtain family genealogy information. Mom, always the storyteller, loved to talk about her relatives, her memories of visiting their homes, what their personalities were like, and anything else she could remember. Mom told Valerie that she'd also be helping me, from the other side, on future genealogy work.

What amazed me even more was that Mom's spirit chose my genealogy work, of all topics, to make her connection to me. After all, there were many other shared events she could have described. But, that very afternoon at home, I had pulled all the notebooks and binders out of the closet, and reviewed my genealogy information on the computer. It was the first time, in over a year, that I had "found the time" to return to this favorite hobby. There was still one branch of the family that needed lots of research and work (Mom's mother's side). Before her death she had told me, several times, she hoped I would work on that family branch some day. I had even ordered microfilms for that family branch earlier that very day. So, for Mom to choose my genealogy work, and for her comment that she'd be helping, had great significance. It seemed to be an acknowledgement that she had been with me, in my home, that afternoon.

Then, Valerie said, "You have a connection to shells, don't you?" I told her that I have always loved shells and have many scattered throughout my home. She nodded, and said, "They have great meaning to you."

Now, I had a second reference to what happened that afternoon at home. It seemed to be a typical Saturday for me (until Valerie's reading, that is). While I was looking for my genealogy information, I noticed a brandy snifter on a bookshelf, full of old, dusty seashells. I had a thought about throwing them away, and said to myself "no way, those mean too much to you." These shells are from many vacations, and day trips to the beach, and I do cherish them. I never really understood why I was so attracted to shells, as I was a farm girl and had not even seen an ocean beach until we stepped on the sand on our honeymoon in the Bahamas. But for some reason, I simply love seashells, of all shapes and sizes.

So not only did I have a quick visit from my mother, I also had an affirmation that God/Spirit, and my ancestors, are with me all the time. Two instances from earlier that day, both thoughts and actions, were mentioned. Both instances held so much meaning for me – my genealogy work and my love of shells. I was blown away!

In the course of the two-hour event, my reading might have seemed insignificant, as it was only a few minutes. I doubt if any of the other participants even remember it. The major event of the evening was the healing for the grieving parents. No one in the room was left untouched by the visit from their son.

However, as I thought more and more about the reading throughout the next days and weeks, the significance grew for me. Valerie referred to three different things in my life that had great meaning for me – pennies, genealogy, and shells.

The appearance of the pennies had just begun in the previous few years, and many of the pennies "appeared" during Mom's terminal illness. Mom and I had many bumps in our relationship over the years. Many of our discussions had ended up in arguments, as I was always trying to help her out of her depressed and unhappy moods. It seemed I'd lost my "real" mother when my father died, as she grieved her loss in various unhealthy ways. When she was diagnosed with lung cancer, her loving ways began resurfacing, and I grieved the loss of my "good" mother, all over again. It was a sad time, but also a blessed time, as we nine adult children were graced with her loving presence, once again. Throughout those trying months, it seemed a penny would show up, just when I needed an emotional lift.

The genealogy work was always a safe area where Mom and I experienced many good times together. We shared fun and laughter, and no arguments occurred. She enjoyed telling me family stories, and I enjoyed receiving the information. Both of us became excited when I made a connection to a new family branch, or found a new, interesting fact. Most of my happy memories of her, in the last fifteen years of her life, were related to my genealogy work. The last time we visited her in her room in the nursing home in Indiana, we shared our pictures of our recent trip to the small villages in France, where we met distant relatives. She shared in my excitement, as she tried to absorb the stories, through her somewhat confused mind.

So, Mom's spirit showing Valerie the scene of us walking through cemeteries was an affirmation to me, from Mom, that she also recognized the importance of the good times between us. It felt as if she reached out to me to express her love and appreciation of the good experiences we had shared during our time together on earth.

And, I pondered the significance of seashells in my life. I realized I purchased my first shell, a large conch shell, on our honeymoon. All the other shells were from family excursions to beaches, whether on a warm, summer afternoon on a Rhode Island beach when we lived there, or on a family vacation. To me, shells were a symbol of never-ending love – love from my husband, my children, and God. I always felt enveloped by calming peace at the beach. I always felt the power and infinity of God through huge waves and far-off horizons. Looking through my collection of shells always evoked peaceful and loving emotions.

Most importantly, the brief reading helped me to feel less separated from my deceased parents. I felt truly connected to them, as I realized our family belief that Dad and Mom watch over all of us could REALLY be true. I realized that if my great-grandmothers are with me, and one of them is leaving me pennies when I feel upset, then all my ancestors support and love me. I realized my genealogy work was more than just an interesting hobby. It was a method of building bridges to stay connected with them – it would be easier to feel that connection if you knew their names and where, and how, they had lived. I had never seen it that way before. I was connected to all of them – and being from a large Catholic family, there are many relatives who love me and are supporting me. There is a unity between us – the living relatives and our deceased relatives.

Within the next few months, I attended several other programs at the same bookstore. I went to another gallery reading night with Valerie, when another co-worker asked me to go with her, so she would not have to attend alone. So I agreed. I went with no expectations at all. Since I had a reading the previous time, which was meaningful to me, I wanted my co-worker to have an equally fulfilling experience.

Valerie was disappointed that only four people were in the audience, and she commented that usually when there is such a small gathering, her readings would not take very long. She stated she would probably spend more time educating us about the Spirit World. The opposite happened. It seemed all our ancestors came through, happy to have less competition for time, and happy to reconnect with the four of us.

Valerie began the session by lowering her head and asking for a blessing on the evening. She raised her head, looked directly at me, and said, "Your Dad's here." She described him perfectly, just as he had looked in a favorite photograph of my Mom's, the day they attended a Hank Williams' concert while they were dating. Valerie described his white t-shirt with a pack of cigarettes rolled up in his sleeve, and the smile on his face.

Then, she would move onto another person, give them a reading, and then Dad would be back! This happened three or four times, and it became comical to the small group. One time, he brought a number of his siblings, his mother, and her favorite dog, Toby. Another time, two of my mother's boyfriends made appearances. Dad came back, laughing, and said he was okay with them showing up that evening. Valerie commented that my father was having a great time connecting with me in this way.

Valerie noted Dad had a very strong presence and asked how long it had been since he passed. When I answered it had been over 30 years, she replied that made sense because spirits often become stronger, the longer they are on the other side. She relayed my father wanted me to be assured that he is with me, as well as with all of my siblings often.

While we laughed, and cried, throughout the evening, it was also very reassuring to me. While Dad had no specific message for me, the fact he was having so much fun connecting to me was truly healing. The small group enjoyed his frequent interruptions and the parade of people he brought with him. My friend also had several relatives come through for her, including her grandmother with whom she'd had an especially close relationship. She felt as stunned as I did.

The strong appearance of my father started an avalanche of further healing for me. I acknowledged how deeply I missed the presence of him in my life. But, more importantly, I realized how he had never really left me. It seemed he was excited about my new openness to mediumship so that he could communicate with me. I loved feeling connected to him, and I wondered if I would be a conduit of messages from him to my siblings. I realized that he really did know what was occurring in our lives – he even knew the guys Mom dated after his death!

I realized that everyone is united in life and in death. There really is no separation between loved ones, whether they still lived on earth, or whether they had crossed over from this life. I no longer felt alone. There is no separation between our loved ones, whether they are still living on earth or in spirit. I felt like a student, learning another lesson!

In my childhood, and at times in my adult life, I had often felt alone and isolated. It seemed I did not fit in anywhere some days. Dad's death had had a traumatic impact on me, as I realized people I love, and am loved by, can simply be gone in an instant. I felt separated from him, and this only amplified the separation I had always felt from the physically healthy, active people in the world. I could not talk to my Dad any more - nor could I participate in a pick-up game of softball. While the effects of my polio and Dad's death may seem like two dissimilar events, the emotions resulting from each of them were similar - separation and isolation.

Although my siblings and I always said we believed Dad was around us, this was proof-positive, he is around all of us. He gave so much relevant information during the event, proving he knew things that occurred shortly after his death, and recently, thirty years later. In essence, he had never really left! We were still united in Spirit. If that was true, I was also united to my mother, and to all my other deceased relatives. I was never alone at all. This truth had always been available to me, but I had not understood the reality of it.

More emotional healing occurred for me, around the relationship with my mother, although she did not appear that evening. Knowing that Dad was aware of her life on earth, after his death, was comforting to me. There had been many, many times when her sharp words had wounded me deeply. Although my psychotherapy training helped me to understand that her words were rooted in her own unhappiness and despair, the words still hurt. Dad had seen all of it, for me and my siblings, and he had loved us and supported us, through all those bad times. The knowledge of Dad's eternal support began to heal the deep hurts within me. I started to release them, eventually forgiving my mother for all the hurtful things she had said to me.

Also, I thought more about the healing Mom had certainly experienced since her death. I knew she had already found more peace and love in the short time since her death, than she had experienced in the last thirty years of her earthly life. I believed her being reunited with her one true love, my father, was what she had been waiting for, for many years. Although her life was full of conflicts and confusion; Dad, and her deceased loved ones had supported her. It is sad that she did not recognize, or feel, their support – it had been there all along for her.

I made many connections to my "old" Catholic beliefs. If I believed in angels, the saints, the Blessed Virgin Mary, and God the Father, Jesus the Son and the Holy Spirit, and believed that I could talk to them through prayer, then why couldn't it be possible to communicate with deceased loved ones? The more I thought about it, the less of a stretch it became. And, if they knew what was going on in my life, could they find joy in my joy? Could they give me comfort in the difficult times? Could they help me in daily struggles, just by sending me their love and support? So many new thoughts to ponder....

My mind and heart became more open to topics that had been virtually unknown to me. I continued to pursue further knowledge through reading, discussing topics with like-minded friends and attending programs at this bookstore. I read books by such authors as Louise Hay, Carolyn Myss, and Doreen Virtue.

There was a great amount of emotional healing for me as I considered new possibilities as to why my life circumstances were what they were. It was a great adventure to explore this whole new world.

Sometimes, though, the new world was not all that different from my more traditional beliefs. After all, Louise Hay describes how emotional and spiritual imbalances affect physical health. And the importance of balance was a favorite theme of mine that I frequently introduced to clients in therapy sessions. When clients present with physical ailments, there are often emotional components lying underneath them.

Carolyn Myss devotes a major part of one book to the sacredness of "sevens," a number that seems to have significance in all major religions. I grew up with the Catholics' seven Sacraments. Doreen Virtue explores the angel world – and Catholics have strong traditional beliefs in angels. I have always believed in angels and had frequently talked to my guardian angel as a child. These were not new concepts to me. It tickled me that so many Catholics, Christians, and non-Christian religious people are fearful of the "new spiritualism," – and yet, many of the beliefs are shared by all. There is a unity between all truths and faith traditions. Perhaps, this should be a lesson for all of us - all peoples of different religions, spiritual and cultural beliefs. It's a pity we often fail to recognize it.

The connectedness that I started to recognize and acknowledge reaffirmed my feelings of unity with all people, and all belief systems. Loneliness and isolation can never exist when connectedness to all people is a reality. Slowly, slowly, my belief system was changing. The lonely little girl with polio was starting to fade away, and a healthier, happier woman was emerging.

Lesson #6: Our loved ones, in spirit, continue to love and support us.

CHAPTER 7

HEALING

In the Spring of 2003, one of my friends in Pittsburgh told me about a spiritual healer from out of state, named Angela. She was coming to the Body, Mind and Spirit Conference in Pittsburgh a few weeks later. Angela does spiritual counseling and physical healing work and offers individual healing sessions. Because my friend knew several people who saw Angela the previous year and thought she was helpful, I decided to give her a try. My openness to new experiences was certainly expanding, as this is something I would have never considered previously.

Although I had no expectations on the session and no idea about what would happen, I assumed it would probably not be unlike a Reiki session. I was beginning to pay attention to suggestions when it seemed further physical healing could be a result. It seemed every time I tried a new venture, good things happened. I was realizing there was a whole new world out there about which I knew very little. I was starting to pay attention and saying "yes" to exciting opportunities.

When I walked into Angela's hotel room, she greeted me warmly and put me at ease immediately. She asked a few questions about why I had decided to schedule the session, and I told her about the fatigue I was still experiencing as a result of my post-polio symptoms. I explained the fatigue had decreased significantly and the leg and knee pain was now gone, as a result of the healing Reiki treatments I had been receiving. She was happy to hear I was using Reiki and supported my continued use of it. This question-and-answer period lasted only a few minutes, and she did not ask for any details about the polio, nor any questions about my profession or family.

She explained that I would lie down on the bed, fully clothed, and she would place her hands on my legs. She said that healing energy comes through her hands, not unlike Reiki energy. She began with a silent meditation, and I felt the strong warmth as soon as her hands touched my legs.

Her first question was, "What is your strongest emotion about having polio?", and I responded, with no hesitation, "sadness." She acknowledged this response, stating Spirit had given her two words about me - self-limitation and deprivation. She commented these two thoughts are forming my belief system and my life, and my life does not have to be defined in these terms.

She continued that I have the belief my symptoms could not change. Instead, I had the opportunity to improve physically over the next years, not get worse as statistics about post-polio syndrome have indicated. It was important to remember all the blessings in my life, and to get rid of any negative thoughts as soon as they come into my mind. She reminded me that I am very, very blessed.

She said new things and new ideas would come into my life that could improve my condition, but I had to believe, really believe, that getting better was a possibility. She affirmed that I was doing many good, healthy things to take care of myself, and I needed to continue on that path.

The first belief that I needed to accept was that I had actually chosen polio for this lifetime, as my soul needed further growth to learn several more life lessons. Then she said this would be my last difficult life on earth, as I would learn all the necessary life lessons this time. When she made that statement, my heart fluttered, and I felt the truth of that statement deep within me.

As if that was not enough, her next statement really startled me! She said that one of the main reasons I had chosen polio was for the benefit of my mother. She asked if my mother had died recently (it was less than a year after Mom's death). She noted three life lessons my mother needed to learn during this lifetime – humility, compassion, and less self-centeredness. She explained the humility was connected to the embarrassment that Mom felt about my handicap.

Mom was not embarrassed about how I looked, she continued, but rather how she perceived the illness to be a reflection of her own unworthiness. I knew immediately what the meaning of this statement was. Mom had mentioned to me several times she believed God was punishing her by giving her a handicapped child. She thought other people probably judged her poorly, as a "bad mother." She had felt guilty and shamed by my affliction. While this is a foreign concept to me, it was very real for her. Later in her life, this belief of hers was further reinforced by the deaths of my baby sister and Dad. Unfortunately, she had the belief that when bad things happened to a person, God was punishing the person for the wrongs they had done.

Angela continued that the amount of time Mom needed to spend with me during the first years of my polio helped her to become less self-centered. And there were times when she felt frustrated by this reality. I immediately remembered some of the negative comments Mom had made to me, as a young child, about her needing to help me with my leg exercises and other activities for my benefit.

Most importantly, I felt an affirmation of my old childhood belief – I had made the choice to have polio. It is hard to explain why this belief is so reassuring to me, except in some way I did have a voice and chose the illness, for a worthy purpose, before I was born. Somehow knowing that I had made the choice, and was not merely a victim of a terrible disease, gives me strength and comfort. It gives meaning and purpose to a situation that seemed to negatively affect every part of my life.

Angela then described the blessedness in my life further. She commented that I have a very solid marriage, and we would experience many more blessings in our life together. She talked about my husband, seeing a possible career change for him. It could be full -time, or it could be part-time, in addition to his being an engineer. She saw that he "just wants to help people," and this is a sign of his spiritual growth.

What she did not know was that Gary was seriously considering becoming a massage therapist. Engineering was no longer fulfilling to him. Many times during the past few years, he'd stated to me, "I just want to help people."

She also told me that my role as a manager was fine for now, but that I needed to consider working directly with people again, especially ill people. I had been having thoughts about leaving my management position to work for a hospice agency in direct patient care. My mother had hospice services for the last six months of her life. Several times, while I watched their wonderful staff, I had thought hospice work would be a fulfilling career change for me.

She stated the two of us are "walking in light" and God will take care of us. She also saw a relocation to an area that is spiritually open, with a warmer climate and more sunshine – another change that my husband and I had been discussing in recent months. She stated the spiritual openness in the community, positive energy in the area, and sunlight would be helpful aspects in further physical healing for me. She stated, several times, that I could experience more healing.

I simply needed to work with God and Jesus to be healed. She also instructed me to call upon the power of the Holy Spirit to assist me in this life journey. She said that I was not tapping into all the Power that is surrounding me. And my old belief system was the only thing preventing deeper healing.

Several times, she stated Gary and I have a very blessed life, with the best years yet to come.

The whole session was absolutely surreal to me. The suggestion that I could get better physically was mind-boggling.

And, my choosing polio to learn life lessons for Mom, and for myself, gave me goose bumps.

Her comments about Gary possibly changing careers were certainly a reference to his state of mind. Reiki was also opening his mind and heart, and he was considering a second career that would be more fulfilling to him than engineering had been. He had been looking into the possibility of massage therapy school and had already talked to several "older" massage therapists who had moved into this field, as a second career. What an affirmation that he was on the right path. Then, there were her comments about my returning to direct patient care.

I remember coming home, still in a state of semi-shock, sitting on our sofa, relating this session to Gary. He was as stunned as I was. I wrote down everything I could remember her saying, and all of my emotional reactions to her words.

Could I really get a lot better physically? I was already quite pleased with my lessening fatigue and the realignment of my knee. I no longer visualized myself spending my later years in a wheelchair. I was doing Reiki every day and practicing yoga on a regular basis.

The possibility of further healing became real to me through this session, and during my journaling afterwards. Prior to the session, I thought it was possible I had already reached the summit of physical improvements. Now I realized I was just beginning on my path, and there could be more physical changes ahead for me.

The connections of healing all levels of my being – mind, body, and spirit – were made during the session with Angela. She pointed out that my belief system – the thoughts in my mind – was the only thing preventing further healing of my body. She also talked about connecting with God the Father, Jesus, and the Holy Spirit, and accessing the Power to heal aspects of myself. Reiki had already opened that pathway to me – and it was no coincidence that Angela also used a hands-on healing technique with me.

All I really had to do was truly believe in the possibility of healing. I simply needed to change my thoughts and follow the opportunities that God would place upon my path. I felt very, very blessed, and started to believe (but not totally convinced) Gary and I had our best days ahead of us.

Lesson #7: Healing is always a possibility in our lives.

CHAPTER 8

LEARNING MEDITATION

There is a feeling that I have when one of these mind-boggling events happen. It is a surreal type of sensation, almost as if I rose out of my body and am floating in the heavens. I almost cannot believe what I just heard. At the same time, there is a resonance in my heart that everything I heard is absolutely true. I feel truth in my bones, in the essence of my being. I feel connected to Spirit when there is a validation of my earthly existence and the connection to my spiritual self.

When Angela talked to me about my choosing to have polio, this statement felt true, although somewhat strange. In order to believe that I had the opportunity to make such a choice, I also had to accept that we are alive before we are born and and that we make choices about our next life. This is part of the belief system of reincarnation. In other words, our souls have many challenging life lessons to learn, and we choose circumstances in the next life to help us learn those lessons. I had already read several books on reincarnation and had some familiarity with this belief, but had not been challenged to either accept, or reject, the belief of reincarnation. I had simply been curious and found reincarnation to be an interesting way to look at life. Not to mention, of course, the Catholic Church teaches that any belief in reincarnation is false – although there is some evidence that reincarnation was accepted in the earliest centuries of the Church. During most of my life, I had accepted current Church teachings on this subject.

Yet, my heart knew the truth of Angela's statements, and it made me feel very excited and happy. I especially enjoyed her comment that I may choose to come back to earth again, but the next life would be easier and would be altruistic, solely for the purpose of serving others. The idea of living an easier life of service was certainly appealing.

This session also caused me to spend hours further analyzing the purpose of my relationship with my mother. While it had not been an easy relationship, it became more palatable in my mind, knowing that both of us learned many life lessons through our struggles. Identifying a purpose to the hurts and emotional distance, such a major part of our relationship during my adolescent and adult years, gave me great peace. I prayed that she too has found some understanding and peace on the other side. It seemed that peace had eluded our relationship during her time on earth.

Prayer had always been a part of my life, living in a Catholic environment. It generally was a one-way street – me asking, pleading, thanking God – for a variety of blessings in my life. What I was less skilled at, honestly, was simply listening to God for guidance and direction. Meditation slowly became a part of my life. We experienced several yoga teachers who were less concerned about physical achievements and more focused on connecting with Spirit. These teachers started classes with each person silently stating an intention, and ending classes with ample time for meditating on that intention.

Journaling became a higher priority for me, as I found so many new things to ponder, with all the Reiki sessions and other extraordinary events that were occurring. Many times, new insights came to me during the writing, and I would sit, in stillness, with those new thoughts. And, my commitment to reading more about these new ways of thinking led me to more meditation.

While meditation is somewhat similar to prayer, there is a basic difference. Meditation can be described as "being" and prayer as "doing." Or, you could say meditation is not using thoughts and words, and prayer is using thoughts and words.

Meditation is not better than prayer, nor vice versa. In our society, however, it seems prayer is more comfortable for most of us, and meditation is practiced less frequently. One can say prayers while driving a car or riding the subway; it is impossible, and certainly not safe, to be in a meditative state during those activities.

Meditation can be experienced as a quieting of our thought processes, simply being with Spirit. It is not easy to quiet our busy, chattering minds, but we can train ourselves to turn off those thoughts. The best way to do that is to acknowledge a thought when it comes to you, and then release it. It is not following the natural progression of one thought leading to another. When practiced frequently, meditation can lead a person to a higher level of consciousness, a place of total connection with Spirit, often called enlightenment.

Prayer can be a powerful communication between God and a person, whether the person uses a formal prayer, or talks to God in an informal conversational mode. Prayer is said to have its greatest power when done together by a community of believers. Generally, a community uses formal prayers that have been memorized by the community, or are written in a book.

Being Catholic, formal prayers within the Church were very comfortable to me, and there are still many times when words fail me, and repeating a familiar Hail Mary or Our Father gives me solace. Practicing meditation on a regular basis was a new experience for me. At first, it seemed meditation was simply "doing nothing," and what was the value in that? But soon, I started to realize the richness of simply disconnecting from my earthly concerns to become connected to Spirit. The more I connected to the loving energies of the spiritual realm, the calmer and more balanced my life became. I was living more frequently in oneness with Spirit and becoming less concerned with earthly happenings.

So, my session with Angela led me to even more meditation. And, when I spent time journaling, I found many new aspects and thoughts to consider. It seemed whenever my spirituality grew in a new direction, my life became enriched in new ways. Another shift occurred for Gary and me.

Through meditation and prayer, Gary made the decision to embark on a second career, and I fully supported it. He enrolled in an excellent massage therapy school that offered weekend courses – two 8-hour days, every other weekend, for two full years. It was a very busy and exciting time for him, as he was energized by the coursework and the opportunities to learn massage by practicing on classmates and friends. It also enabled me to have many free hours to further pursue my own spiritual growth, through reading, journaling and meditation, and attending more workshops and classes. Our lives were changing rapidly.

Lesson #8: We can learn how to connect to Spirit.

CHAPTER 9

SYNCHRONICITIES AND SIGNS

Traveling is one of the great loves of my life. While we have visited many places, there are still so many more to see. Before Gary's massage therapy classes started, we decided to travel to the Carolinas. Our first stop was Charleston, South Carolina, a beautiful city we had never visited. I wanted to see one of the in-town plantations, and our tourist book stated if you only had time for one, this was the plantation to see. Upon our arrival, the ticket seller stated a tour had started a few minutes earlier, but we could join the group in the parlor. The guide was in the middle of relating the family history, and soon two other couples also joined the tour. When the guide finished this portion, she commented she'd be happy to bring us three couples back into the parlor, after the tour, to review any historical information we may have missed.

The tour ended in the lovely outside courtyard, and the seven of us returned to the parlor to hear the entire family history. We had to wait in the hallway until the next tour group finished in the parlor. The guide asked Gary and me where we were from, and when we replied Pittsburgh, she smiled and said she and her husband had lived there once. In fact, it was her favorite city where they had lived, and they had relocated many times, due to his career.

I asked what part of Pittsburgh they had lived in, and she said North Hills. I replied we also live in that part of the city – and I continued with the questions – where did they live in North Hills? What development? What street? Yes, you guessed it – they actually had lived in our development, and on our street! So, of course, I had to ask the next question, what house had they owned? Much to our great astonishment, they had lived in our house – in fact, they were the first owners of it! The seven of us stood there, in total disbelief. What were the chances? Soon, she was asking us questions about the neighbors, and we told her about some of the home improvements we had made. Then, it was time to go into the parlor to complete the tour. After the tour was complete, we shared more information with each other, and then, we were on our way.

After the tour, Gary and I had dinner and discussed what the meaning of this "coincidence" could be. So many small things had to happen for this coincidence to occur – we had to miss the beginning of the tour; the guide had to choose us, among the three couples, to ask where we were from; I had to ask the right questions, etc. The explanation that resonated with us that evening was this was a revelation of how God works. He gives us signs that He is always with us, and sometimes, the signs may be subtle and easy to miss. However, there are other times when He gets our attention in big ways - and meeting the person who'd owned our house was one of those times. I'd always loved the saying that "coincidences are God's way of staying anonymous."

This is an example of a synchronicity – God lining up many details to grab our attention, or to teach us a lesson. God uses synchronicities to remind us we are on the right path and are finding our life's purpose. We are given signs and coincidences to remind us that Spiritual Guidance is with us, every step of the way. When we recognize these signs, the Universe sends us more. Common affirmations from the Universe include rainbows, falling stars, and feathers, but there are also many more signs made available to us.

God also participates by sending us small miracles, and we know our prayers have been answered. Miracles can be created by anyone who is connected to Divine Source. Many doctors, nurses, and other health care workers have their own stories of how prayers miraculously changed the course of a life-threatening situation turning into a successful healing. There are now numerous research studies demonstrating the power of prayer in the medical setting, and there are many inspiring books relating these stories.

A few years later, I read a book that added to my understanding of coincidences, and introduced me to a deeper understanding of synchronicity. The book is "Synchronicity and You" by Frank Joseph. Here is his explanation of the true meaning of these signs:

"The term synchronicity was coined by one of the twentieth century's most influential thinkers, the Swiss psychologist Carl Gustav Jung. He defined synchronicity as any apparent coincidence that inspires a sense of wonder and personal meaning or particular significance in the observer. It is a perceived connection between two or more objects, events, or persons without any recognizable cause."

I revisited the story of the Charleston coincidence and derived a deeper message for Gary and me. The true message of this synchronicity for us was to trust God in our new and revised life path. We would be taken care of, and everything would work out fine. Although I had supported Gary's choice to change careers, I had to admit this decision was also somewhat scary for me. I had always assumed he would stay with his well-paid, dependable career as an engineer until retirement. That assumption gave me a feeling of security. I knew that developing a solid clientele base in massage therapy would take time, and our income could be greatly affected. At the same time, I also believed that if Gary's life purpose was to be a massage therapist, God would take care of us.

This synchronicity gave me reassurance then, and it continues to be my reassurance any time I feel unsure of our financial situation. It has served to build confidence and trust in our chosen paths.

As time went on, I began to remember other synchronicities

that had occurred in my life. While I knew these synchronicities were more than just mere coincidences at the time they occurred, I did not realize the full significance of them. I took the time to fully study them and recognize the true meanings. Because the Charleston event was so astounding, I decided it was time to give more attention to other past events. I wrote down every incident I could remember in detail, what else was going on in my life at the time, and discerned what the true messages were. These events became more meaningful to me, and I realized how many opportunities God had given me to understand His love and assistance in my life. I had failed to read the signs.

One amazing synchronicity that I recalled occurred many years earlier, in the early 90s. I had not given it any kind of spiritual meaning then, but I certainly do now. Although I was always an avid reader, I had read very little in the metaphysical arena up to that time. A friend had been encouraging me to read a certain book for at least a year, called *Many Lives, Many Masters* by Brian Weiss, M.D. Dr. Weiss is a psychiatrist whose client revealed several past lives while in a hypnotic state. He has since become an expert in the field of past life regression therapy.

Because I was headed out of town to attend a diabetes education conference (this was when I was a hospital social worker working with children with diabetes), I went to my local library to find a book for the flight. I remembered my friend's recommendation and found Dr. Weiss' book. I started reading it that evening. In fact, I read into the wee hours, as I could not put the book down.

The next morning, I sent our kids off to school and flipped on the television set while packing. Guess who was on the talk show? Yes, it was Dr. Weiss, talking about past life regression therapy. With him was an actress from a daytime soap opera, and she disclosed she had sought treatment from Dr. Weiss. She stated she had always had severe neck pain and had sought many medical treatments over the years, with no success. She'd heard about Dr. Weiss and decided to give his work a try. During the first past life regression therapy session, she recalled a previous life when she died in a house fire, as a beam fell from the ceiling, striking the back of her neck, instantly killing her. Amazingly, she reported that her neck pain disappeared during the session and has never returned.

During the flight, I finished the book. Upon arrival in my hotel room, I reviewed the conference program and could not believe my eyes. One of the presenters was the actress whom I'd seen on television earlier in the day with Dr. Weiss! She has a son with diabetes and had written a book about her experience of raising a child with this disease (this information had not been shared on the television show). Of course, I had to attend her session. After her session and book-signing was finished, I was able to spend a few minutes alone with her. I told her that I had seen her on the talk show the previous day, and we discussed her therapy session and how helpful past life regression therapy had been to her.

At that time, I saw how "coincidental" these events were. But I did not have the knowledge at that stage of my spiritual development to discern significant meaning from the synchronicity. Now, the message for me is that reading and learning more about the spiritual realm is an important, and necessary, part of my life journey. I am a student on earth, learning many life lessons.

We do receive affirmations when we are on the right path – we simply have to be aware enough to see them. We must give frequent gratitude for these synchronicities, as the more we acknowledge and thank God for these signs, the more we will receive.

The third story was truly a sign from God. I get goose bumps just thinking about it! When Gary and I decided to attend the Reiki training, it was a stretch for us, as we had always been a couple with traditional beliefs and practices. Learning Reiki was totally different from anything we had ever done. We felt excited, and nervous.

That Friday morning, both of us went to our jobs, as usual. But a very unusual occurrence happened during my drive to work. I always listened to the same radio station, but that morning, I felt restless and started to search through channels. I happened to find a station where two guests, women who receive messages from the deceased and from angels, were talking to callers. I was fascinated by every message received for each caller. Some of the messages came from family members who had died, and others were from angels, providing guidance for present circumstances. All the messages were specific and detailed.

Then, something odd happened. A new caller asked a question, and it seemed everything the women said, did not fit. One of them finally said, "He is your father who has passed and is trying to communicate with you. His name is Jim." The caller replied, no, my father's name is Daniel, and he is living. Then, the other woman responded, "Do you know a Roy that has passed?" Again, the caller responded with a no. The woman again asked, "Are you sure you don't know a Jim, or a Roy, who has passed?" and the caller firmly replied no. Both women confirmed the message was very clear, so it had to be a message for someone else, perhaps the next caller, or perhaps for a listener.

I was listening to this entire conversation in stunned silence. Jim Roy was my father's name! Was it just a coincidence? Was it a sign from him? Since it happened the morning of our first Reiki training weekend, could it be his approval that we were embarking on this new journey? This seemed like too much of a coincidence, to be merely an insignificant incident.

At work, I told two of my more open-minded coworkers this story, and both had the same reaction. Both said it was my Dad saying "hi," and it was his affirmation that Reiki would be important to us. This was yet another sign that Dad was still involved in my life and was approving of my journey.

Affirmations can be given by our ancestors too. And, the ways they find to communicate with us can be heartwarming, and fun. It was an amazing start to an amazing weekend. Dad was blessing our Reiki weekend, as he knew that we were starting down a new and exciting road of learning.

So many amazing things were happening in my life. It seemed I was learning lots of new information, and everything was working together, hand-in-hand. I simply had to learn to recognize and appreciate these signs, and amazing things happened.

Lesson #9: Synchronicities are God's way of getting our attention!

CHAPTER 10

BECOMING INTENTIONAL

Valerie, the psychic medium who had already played an important role in the expansion of my beliefs, continued her role in my spiritual growth. She also offers Psychic Development Classes to those who were interested in further developing their intuitive abilities. Since Gary was busy many weekends with his massage therapy training, it was easy for me to find time to attend her classes.

The classes included a few people who thought they may become professional mediums. But, most of the attendees were like me – curious students who wanted to learn more about intuitive abilities and see if they could develop their own sixth sense. Although everyone has a sixth sense, most people do not acknowledge it, attempt to become comfortable with it, or develop it.

I was beginning to live more intentionally. I set the intention to learn more about my intuitive abilities and pursued opportunities to fulfill the intention. A few stepping stones had been placed on my path of further spiritual growth. My path had always been a more traditional, religious one, and I still maintained it. But, in addition, I made the intentional decision to explore other possibilities. Reiki, the synchronicities, the possibilities of getting better physically, connecting with my ancestors, understanding my connection with God in new and exciting ways – there was a whole new world out there for me to explore. Once the intention was formed in my mind, and I took the actions to make it happen, more wonderful incidents occurred.

For one of our classes, Valerie instructed us to bring a picture of someone in our life who had transitioned to the other side. We did not give any information about the person to the others, simply placed our photos in a pile, picture sides down, not knowing who had brought each picture. Valerie asked each of us, one by one, to choose a picture, turn it over, and gaze into the person's eyes. Then, each of us shared what we had intuited.

I felt nervous and unsure about this exercise, as I chose my photograph. When I turned it over, I saw a colored snapshot of an older gentleman. It looked like a photo from the 1960s, taken during the Christmas holidays. He was staring into the camera, and I looked into his eyes. Thoughts and feelings flooded into my mind. Much to my amazement, I intuited his complex personality. When it was my turn to share, I stated it seemed the gentleman in the photo was a complex man, almost as if he had two personalities. I saw a logical, down-to-earth man, who often felt uncertain, had a lack of confidence about himself, and was confused about his life. But, he also had a gregarious, humorous side, and was well-liked. It seemed as if he had lived a very complicated life. I felt his love for his family, but it seemed there were times he was unable to show his love. A class member stated that I had described her alcoholic father to a tee. This was proof-positive to me that anyone can learn to hone intuitive skills!

Another evening, Valerie taught us about the Akashic Records. Akashic Records contain every single life event, from all our multiple past lives. These records are stored in the Spirit World and are accessible to us, if approached for the right purpose – for the highest good. Spirit may choose to show us a scene from a previous life when a lesson would be beneficial to us now, in our current life.

Valerie guided us through a visualization exercise. She asked us to close our eyes and take several deep breaths, and set the intention to receive a message that would be beneficial to us at the present time. We were asked to visualize the Temple of Akashic Records from the outside, walk up the steps, through the door, and walk down the center aisle. When we reached the area where our individual record is stored, we would be guided to turn down the correct aisle, and stop in front of our own book. We set the intention to open the book to a page that showed a scene from a previous lifetime, a scene where a message that we needed to hear now, could be given to us. Her guidance made this exercise easy to do. I saw myself, walking along the main aisle and turning down the correct side aisle. I gently turned pages of a large book, until I knew it was time to stop.

What I saw was myself as a young, beautiful woman playing the piano, in a well-appointed home. The piano was placed by large windows facing a garden, and two candelabra, resting on a lacy scarf, graced the top of the piano. I was wearing a long, full-skirted, gold-colored dress, printed with large flowers. I remember noticing the similarity between this flowered fabric with a dress in my closet at home with a similar floral design. Valerie instructed us to ask the year, and I was told it was 1824.

Feelings of sadness and loneliness overwhelmed me, and the music I was playing mirrored my sad mood. We were further instructed to ask questions about the scene – What was happening? Why is this past life experience important to me now? What is the lesson I need to learn for this lifetime?

Answers to these questions flowed into my mind. My husband had died, and I was very sad. I was told the husband of that lifetime was my father in this lifetime. I was then taken to another scene from 1824, where I had on a long, gray coat, visiting the grave, later that same year. I was told, in my mind, "He is not there." But, I never understood, in that lifetime, that he continued to be with me. And in this life, for most of the years since my Dad's death in 1971, I had not really understood he continued to be with me, in spirit form.

I was told I needed to learn an important life lesson – when someone dies, he remains with you, and you are never alone. The words, "you are never alone," were repeated over and over to me during this exercise.

Suddenly, it became clear to me that during this lifetime, I had often felt those same feelings of sadness and loneliness. Not all those feelings were connected to this lifetime's feelings – rather, they were "left over" from many previous lifetimes. I had chosen to be "different," through the experience of polio, to re-experience those feelings, yet again. And, Dad and I chose together to relive the experience of a family connection, with his leaving this earth early, again. I was overcome with "knowing" that my Dad is still with me in this lifetime. I was told that Dad comes through to me in my dreams all the time, but generally I do not remember those dreams.

I continued to be overcome with feelings, and the flow of tears, as the guided meditation progressed. We were guided back to the present time, and then we wrote about the experience. The meditation experience was as real to me, as the experience of sitting at the computer right now, typing away on this keyboard. My journal entry included the following thoughts:

The piano – what a connection that is! One of my strongest desires as a little girl was to play the piano, but I was always told it was something that my parents could not afford – the piano, nor the lessons. All of us kids loved to watch our Aunt Dory play "Pretty Baby" and other favorites on our Grandma's piano during family gatherings, and my desire to do the same was always very strong.

Farm auctions were, and still are, a common occurrence in rural Indiana. One Saturday, Dad came home with an old piano for us kids to tinker with (although I always secretly believed he bought it for me, as I was the only child expressing the desire to play). I was ecstatic and spent hours on that old upright piano, teaching myself some rudimentary skills. I wanted lessons so bad I could taste it. (By the way, I was finally able to start taking lessons as an adult some twenty years ago.) Now I knew Dad bought that piano because we had had that connection in an earlier lifetime. My arms were covered with goose bumps, and the tears continued to flow.

The Akashic Record exercise gave me many insights into the choices I made prior to and during, this lifetime. The strong, familiar feelings of sadness and loneliness, my old companions, lessened considerably. I became more aware that I am never alone, as I am always surrounded by many Spirits who love me – whether they are relatives from this life or other lives, angels, Spirit Guides, saints, God, the Universe – you name it, all of them are with me. Although Dad left this earth over thirty years ago, he never really left me. "You are never alone" became my new mantra, and it served to deepen my healing. Not only was I healing emotions from this lifetime, but also emotions stored within my soul from many previous lifetimes.

Another evening during the Psychic Development series, Valerie stated that we'd be meeting a Spirit Guide. I was filled with excitement and trepidation. A few months earlier, I had read my first book about Spirit Guides and tried to meet mine, through an exercise in the book. I was disappointed that the exercise did not reveal my Spirit Guide.

The idea of Spirit Guides was a relatively new concept to me, although they are somewhat similar to angels – and I had always believed in angels. Angels have always been spiritual beings and have never lived in human form. Spirit Guides are people who lived on earth at some time, but passed and now live in spirit form. Guides are highly evolved beings who are still very interested in our earthly journeys. They are guides and mentors, prepared to help us, especially when we ask for their assistance. And they help us even when we are not aware of their existence. One way they communicate with us is through inspirational thoughts that all of us have. Unfortunately, we often ignore and dismiss those thoughts as silly, or unworkable.

There can be a "major" Spirit Guide who is with us throughout most of this lifetime, or during several lifetimes.

And, there can be other Spirit Guides who work with us during specific periods of our life journey, and then move on. For me, this was not a huge leap in faith.

That evening, through Valerie's guided exercise, I set the intention of meeting a Spirit Guide who has been with me most of this lifetime. I met Charles. Charles revealed himself to me as a Roman soldier who lived in the 400s A.D. He was dressed in a tunic, with sandals, and leather laces tied around his legs. I am happy to report that Charles is a very handsome guy, with black hair and penetrating black eyes. He is a large, strong man, and the power emanating from deep within his core was palpable.

He told me that he has been with me this entire lifetime, although he had never been a part of my previous lives. He continued to inform me that physical strength had been too important to me before, and this life was to help me balance the old, misguided priority. He also told me that many people in this lifetime had acted powerfully towards me, in a negative way. They had misunderstood the true meaning of power, and I too often felt powerless with them. I also had to learn how to recognize the true power within me. In addition to feeling his strength and power, I also felt unconditional love and protection from him.

That message certainly hit the nail on the head. During the previous few years of my life, I had been seeking, and reinforcing, the power within myself. I had been using Reiki to energize my third chakra, the solar plexus chakra, for some time. The solar plexus chakra emphasizes the power of self, finding one's own inner strength and will.

This kind of power is the opposite of being a victim. It had always been a struggle for me not to feel victimized by polio. I deepened my understanding of this mentality, through my education of becoming a psychotherapist, and by working with many clients who experienced their lives as victims. I learned this mentality is a choice, and I had made great strides in not identifying myself as a victim.

The next step was realizing my own inner strength and power. During this period in my life, I was dealing with another situation that sought to steal my power – my work environment. There were many difficult people in my agency who thrived on being powerful (in the negative sense of the word), and I was learning to stand up to them. It was not easy for me to stand up to authoritative or mean people, to stay firm in my convictions, to state the facts and my opinions, in reasonable and solid ways. During the drive to work each morning, I visualized a sheath of bright light surrounding my body, protecting me from the negative energies that I encountered during the workday. I had intentionally been utilizing positive thoughts to stand strong against the difficult co-workers and to shield myself against the negative energies that surrounded me.

I realized that Charles could assist me (and in fact, he had been all my life) in this work environment. This session added to my belief that everything has a purpose. Meeting Charles at that point in my life was an affirmation that I was moving along my life path just as I was meant to be.

Stating an intention is the first step in manifesting positive occurrences in our lives. It is the process of identifying our desires and stating them clearly. Then intention must be accompanied by energy and action. The purpose of the intention must be for the higher good, not for self-centered or greedy motivations. Making an intentional statement is a powerful step in creating one's reality. It is not ambivalent or weak. It is sending the Universe a clear message – this is my desire and it is for a good purpose. Everyone has the ability to create a life of healing, peace and love, and it begins with thought, followed by an intentional statement. With the right thoughts and intentions, all good things can be manifested.

Lesson #10: We can create purposeful, loving lives through intention.

CHAPTER 11

ATTRACTING POSITIVE ENERGY

It is important to note that most hours of most days, I lived a so-called "normal" life. I went to work, cooked dinner, did the laundry, paid the bills, and so on. I did not live in some la-la land, separate from ordinary life. However, my understanding of this life had shifted considerably, and both my husband and I believed that our best days were yet to come.

Gary completed massage therapy school but he still worked as an engineer. He had joined a newly-formed massage therapy practice in Pittsburgh, but business was slow. I continued to struggle with the difficult personalities in my workplace, but found comfort knowing my staff was providing the highest quality of psychotherapy to the children and families entrusted to our care.

Gary and I decided it was time to start thinking about future plans. Neither of us saw ourselves retiring in Pittsburgh, and we needed to consider where we would want to live. Perhaps we could even move before retirement began. The idea of living in a warmer climate was enticing. We planned two vacations for the spring – one to visit Asheville, North Carolina, and the other to visit Richmond, Virginia. The following year, we could look at other places, with a plan to eventually move, possibly within a few years.

In April, we visited Asheville and fell in love with its beauty, its climate, and its openness to all kinds of people and belief systems. For a city its size, it has a plethora of new age bookstores, spiritual groups, yoga and massage centers – as well as worship sites for many Christian, Buddhist and other major religions. What an interesting combination – it sounded just like us!

After our return to Pittsburgh, we could not get Asheville out of our minds. So, we changed our plans. Rather than driving to Richmond for our second vacation, we decided to return to Asheville to research the job and housing markets in the area. We decided only one of us had to have a job to move.

Before the trip, both of us searched the Internet for job openings. Working for a hospice was still in my heart, and there just happened to be a position for a social worker at a hospice agency near Asheville. I emailed my resume, and I received a phone call to schedule an interview during our vacation week. Both of us strongly believed if this move was meant to be, everything would fall into place. If not, things would not work out, and it would be a sign that this is not the right place or time for us to move.

Yes, I was extended a job offer from the Director of Social Services at the hospice agency. Gary's engineering company offered him the opportunity to telecommute from Asheville. Everything fell into place perfectly. We had no doubts this move was to be the next step in our journey. We surprised our families and friends when we announced we were moving to our pre-retirement city – the following month.

My story, of course, includes my husband's journey as well. His background is even more traditional than mine, and his training as an engineer only reinforced his rational, logical way of thinking. But, there was always a part of him that did not fit the engineering mold. That other side of him started to grow with his Reiki practice and his pursuit of working as a massage therapist. He finds a level of comfort and peace when he does a massage or Reiki, and he was moving towards working with people who have major illnesses or physical conditions.

Those first few months in Asheville were very busy, with buying a house, my getting settled into a new job, and Gary working for his company electronically. Part of our plan was for

Gary to be able to leave the engineering position eventually and work as a massage therapist solely. Through a number of synchronicities, he was handed the opportunity to open a massage therapy business, in a space where three or four practitioners could work simultaneously. Part of the business would be renting these spaces to other massage therapists and healers, and forming a collaborative group of like-minded practitioners. The other part would be income from his providing massages, and both of us would provide Reiki treatments. All the pieces fell into place, and everything went smoother than we could have ever imagined.

Several weeks before the opening of the business, Gary advertised for healing practitioners to rent space from us. One Saturday morning when both of us were at the center preparing for the opening, a woman named Starr came by to look at the space, as a potential renter. She greeted us, took one look at me, and said, "You're having issues with your left hip, aren't you?" My first thought was, "wow, can she really see that kind of energy?" I was leaning against the wall, had not walked in front of her, so it had been not obvious to her that I had any kind of physical disability.

It was just a few weeks after I'd had my first bone scan, and it was found that I had the earliest stages of osteopenia, the precursor to osteoporosis. Oddly, the calcium deficiency was in the left hip only. The calcium levels throughout all my other bones were well above average for a woman my age. The doctor stated it was very odd to find a deficiency in one area only, but it could be related to the fact that my left leg was left weaker by the polio, and I may have "favored" my left side all these years, resulting in this deficiency.

I liked Starr immediately and felt a strong connection to her, as she explained the kind of work she did with clients. She described herself as an intuitive shamanic healer. I knew very little about shamanic healing and had certainly never met this kind of healer before. I had incorrect notions that shamans lived centuries ago, and were wise, old men from other cultures, like Peru, Haiti, or countries in Africa. It was a surprise to me that a young American Caucasian woman could be a shamanic healer. But, her comment about my hip problem amazed me, and I was more than curious. My curiosity led me to ask her a few questions, and a few days later, I scheduled my first shamanic healing session with her.

Even before that first session, Gary and I often discussed the many synchronicities that occurred in our lives once we became open to moving to Asheville. My finding a job in a hospice agency so easily, his opening a massage and healing arts center, our meeting so many other healers – the list went on. As we became more open, the Universe opened up to us, in so many exciting ways.

In recent years, a great deal has been written about attracting positive and negative energies into our lives. The concept is simply this: Like attracts like. We produce and emit vibrations of energy, positive and negative. When we emit positive energies, we attract people into our lives who also emit positive energies. Our energy vibrations were rising, due to our intentions to bring healing to others, through the practice of massage and Reiki, and providing space for other healers. Suddenly, we were surrounded by many positive-energy-charged people, people who had the intention of bringing healing to others.

This concept can also work against us, when we are emitting negative energies, as people with similar negative energy fields will come into our lives. Why did I spend the previous eight years in such a negative work environment (although among positive people in my own department)? It was a mirror into my own being – in some areas, I was emitting positive energy – mentoring my staff, feeling genuine respect for their work, and demonstrating compassion for our clients.

But, in dealing with difficult peers and administrators, I was emitting the negative energy of fear. This fear rose from the core of my being. I felt a strong lack of internal power and self-confidence. I attracted the very behaviors that challenged the core of my inner being. Fortunately, I had taken a good, hard look at these dynamics and knew I needed to make changes to preserve, and encourage growth, of the goodness that lay within me. I had to protect myself from those kinds of harmful energies.

I was certainly open to more healing for myself. In fact, one of the reasons we moved to Asheville was to experience the sunshine and warmer climate to improve my physical energy. An intuitive shamanic healer – why not? When I first heard of Reiki, it seemed pretty "out there" too, and now it was a regular routine in my everyday life. While I felt excitement about experiencing a shamanic healer, I did not have any preconceived ideas, or expectations, about what might happen. I was trusting Spirit would place the right people on my path at the right time, so I moved ahead in faith.

Lesson #11: We attract positive – and negative – energies into our lives.

CHAPTER 12

THE FIRST SESSION

I had no idea what my first session with Starr would be like, nor did I have any idea what a large impact it would have in my healing process.

What do you do? What do you say? What do you wear? My head was filled with many questions, and my body was filled with great anxiety. I felt like I was going on a great adventure, but I had no information or details about it. I did not know what to expect. And, yet, it felt like it was something I simply had to do - something, or Someone, was pulling me in that direction.

My world was literally turned upside down that day. When Starr asked me what I hoped to gain from a session, I told her I really did not know. I explained that I was totally amazed with her ability to detect a problem in my left hip, and so it simply seemed like a good idea. I mentioned my history of polio, in about two sentences, no specifics at all. I told her I was curious about this healing method called intuitive shamanic healing, although I had never read anything about it or barely heard the term before. I was open to whatever would happen.

We sat in chairs facing each other, in a quiet room, with a massage table in it. Starr explained she does not work in any particular shamanic tradition, although she had trained with several traditional shamanic healers. She does not use some of the traditional instruments, like drums or rattles. She simply communicates with Spirit, by closing her eyes and seeing scenes that Spirit shows her, for several minutes. Then, she opens her eyes, describing to the client what she saw and the conversations she'd had with whatever Spirit Guides had come forward. She would alternate between visiting the Spirit World, in silence, and then communicating the scenes and messages to me, in the physical world.

And so, we began.

The first time Starr "left" and "returned," she related quite an unusual scene. She informed me she had been greeted by a little girl, and she struggled in explaining how this little girl appeared, without sounding insensitive. The little girl was very obese, oddly-shaped, and unhappy. The little girl told Starr she felt neglected and unloved by me, and asked that I hold and embrace her.

Starr instructed me to close my eyes and imagine holding this little girl in my arms, and tell her I love her. At the same time I closed my eyes and imagined this scene, Starr went back to Spirit World. When I completed the exercise as instructed, I opened my eyes. Starr reported she saw me hugging the little girl, with genuine emotion. She then saw the little girl return to a normal shape and size, and she happily skipped away, as little girls do.

Starr asked if I had any idea as to what the meaning of this Spirit, and her interaction with me, might be. The meaning was crystal-clear to me. I related to how the girl must have felt, looking so unshapely and grotesque, and stated I'd often felt that way myself, especially when I was a little girl. There are times when I still feel unattractive, in a world of seemingly beautiful women. Both of us saw the need for me to love the little girl within, and reassure her she is beautiful and loved. Within a few minutes, I had already experienced some healing, but there was more to come.

(During the description of the remainder of the session, I will not clearly indicate the going-back-and-forth between the two worlds, but that is the pattern of this work, and the pattern of all my future sessions with Starr.)

When Starr went back to the Spirit World, she and I were led to an African jungle where there was a tribe of dark-skinned people. This tribe greeted me warmly, and it was obvious that I was well-known and cherished by this group of people, although I presented as a pretty, young white woman. Starr laughed while she explained to me how white I looked, as compared to the rest of the tribe! Starr was informed I have been in the process of healing for several years, and more healing was to come into my life, if I was open to the possibility. And this tribe would participate in the healing process. I just needed to trust, and do my part, in the healing process too.

The leader, who was tall and regal-looking, came down from a throne-like chair and also greeted me warmly. He gave specific instructions as to what I needed to do now, in the physical world. He asked me to close my eyes and think about all the shells in my house. He instructed me to select one shell and imagine it being in my hands. I have three conch shells on a bookshelf at home and knew the smallest one was to be the special shell. Right then, I became aware of the strong connection between my current life in the physical world, and the world of Spirit. Spirit knew I had always had an attraction to shells and have many displayed throughout my home.

He also instructed me to buy a journal and start writing. This journaling would eventually become a book, and the book would influence many people around the world. When I wrote, the shell, as well as two other items that would be revealed to me in the near future, would also be with me.

Starr asked him if there was a specific area in my house, or elsewhere, where I was supposed to do this writing. The answer was no, these items would create "sacred space" for my writing. I did not need to designate a particular space or room in my house for this writing, but could take the shell, the other items, and my journal anywhere, such as to a park or on trips, to create the sacred space. Or, I could just visualize the items anywhere, and sacred space would surround me. I would receive guidance and direction during my journaling. The leader also stated if I ever felt stuck and needed more guidance at any point during writing time, I could hold the shell to my ear, and I would receive assistance from the Spirit tribe.

I also needed to buy a second journal, this one would be for "Life Lessons" that would come into my mind over time. It would become a record of inspired thoughts that I could revisit whenever I needed them.

This encounter was stunning, to say the least. This was the second time in my life I was told I'd be writing a book that would influence many people. The first time was at an "angel event" that I attended several years earlier, at the new-age bookstore in Pittsburgh. It was a two-hour program where an "angel lady" (someone who communicates with angels) taught us about angels, how they protect us, guide us, and so on. She went around the packed room and gave a very brief reading to each person. My writing a book some day had been one of the messages she gave me – other messages were more general and less memorable than that one. Hearing it the second time was indeed a strong message.

As you may remember, I'd also received a message about my connection to shells, during my first medium gallery experience. And yes, there are a number of shells displayed throughout my house. There's a shell plaque, a framed shell reading, a large glass container filled with shells from numerous beach outings, shell leis from Hawaii, and three conch shells of varying sizes, from our travels. Intuitively, I knew which shell I was to choose.

He also told Starr to give me a copy of a CD that she has of African drumming music. He told her that music and sound is healing to me, and that I should listen to this CD as often as possible. Any other CD with this type of music could also be beneficial. Most importantly, though, he told Starr that all I needed to do was "remember, remember, remember."

Before the tribal leader left my side, he whispered something into my ear. I, nor Starr, know what it was, on a conscious level; but it made me feel very happy, and I believe this message is still with me, on some unattainable level.

The session lasted about an hour and a half. I knew it was significant, but I did not know exactly what happened, in human terms. On the physical level, I believed that the newly-found osteopenia was on its way to being healed. On an emotional level, I felt I had healed a wounded part of me that had been with me since childhood. On a spiritual level, this session gave me an experience unlike any others I have ever had.

It seemed I was attracting more healing into my life, in ways I had never considered, or barely knew anything about. Although in many ways I was emotionally healthy, I now saw how some parts of me were not yet healed. I made a personal commitment to do more work on my emotional self, and the journaling began.

All in all, I was simply blown away AGAIN. It is one thing to read about surreal experiences – it is another to actually live them! The connection to my real physical life was undeniable. Receiving the message, for a second time, that part of my life's purpose is to write a book to teach people something significant certainly got my attention. That one message, in itself, provided validation to the entire experience. It seemed I had no choice but to respond with trust.

One of my favorite places in our Asheville home is my reading corner in our master bedroom. It would now be my writing corner, too. The next day, I bought my journals. I took my shell off the shelf in the living room and set it next to the journal, on the small table in my reading corner. It seemed I was starting on a new adventure, riding on a whirlwind of excitement. What could possibly happen next?

Lesson #12: Saying "yes" to new opportunities enriches our lives.

CHAPTER 13

BECOMING RESPONSIBLE

Frequently, acquaintances and friends comment how well I have always dealt with my polio. I am a happy, positive person, someone who always smiles, finding joy in daily life. A number of times, friends have told me they almost forget my disability, even as they see me walk with a pronounced limp. It is true, on many levels I am a happy and joyful person. But, remaining were deeper levels of emotions where healing was still needed.

Journaling was not a new concept to me. I have journaled from time to time in my life, usually when I was living through a trying situation, or developing a new insight into an emotional area of my life. In my past therapy work with clients or super-visory work with clinical staff, I often suggested free-writing journaling to assist them in their own life journeys. Free-writing means to simply let the thoughts and feelings flow, with no consideration as to whether the words or sentence structure are grammatically correct, or if there is any logical sense. Many wonderful insights and answers to life's dilemmas can be discovered through free-writing. During my first days of journaling after this session, ideas and thoughts that I had not visited for many years, some since my childhood, resurfaced.

I quickly realized how detached I had become emotionally from my inner child, the little girl who had polio. In our old family album, there are several photographs of me wearing the full-length braces that always made me feel conspicuous and less than pretty. In one picture, I am standing on our front porch, leaning against the window to our living room. In another, I am perched between my two sisters. For as many years as I can remember, when I looked at those pictures, I felt so much sadness and pity for that poor, little girl. But I did not feel sadness for me. It was like looking at a picture of another person. I did not connect with my own feelings when those pictures were snapped, or when I looked at the photos, many years later.

What I realized is that I had become emotionally detached from my little girl, my inner child, as some psychologists call it. I had managed to separate myself, or disconnect myself, from who I was. I had compartmentalized my pain and sadness, locking those feelings in a small treasure chest inside of me and throwing away the key. I worked hard to leave all those emotions behind me, as I developed a happy adult life with a wonderful marriage and children. I needed to reintegrate that part of myself into my whole being, and to embrace the reality of the early years of my life. I gradually became aware it would be important to grow in gratitude for the experience of polio and accept the reality that it served a meaningful purpose in my life and in the lives of people who crossed my path.

Several journal entries dealt with the question of why I had been stricken with polio in the first place. I had not revisited that question for many, many years – and certainly not in depth, since I was a little girl. I have many memories of trying to answer that question when I was very young. Trying to find a reason for contracting the disease gave me some fulfillment and helped me to accept the consequences, even at a very young age. It made sense to me that God had to have a reason, and a good reason at that, to choose me to be stricken with this disease.

Most of my "answers" in my early years focused on how it affected my personality.

Polio made me stronger, more determined and strong-willed. It gave me the opportunity to read and learn, and not be distracted by physical activity. Many times, I overheard the adults say that it was a good thing one of the girls in the family contracted the disease, as it would have been harder for a boy. Farmers' lives were demanding, requiring physical strength. So I thought that God had even chosen the right gender for me to be.

At my first healing session several years earlier in Pittsburgh, a broader purpose was given to me. Polio was part of my life plan to learn my own life lessons, as well as challenge my mother to further develop some positive characteristics. That revelation stretched my understanding of why things happen to us. In my traditional religious upbringing, God's plan for each of us was an accepted belief. As I started to read more books of the spiritual genre, my understanding of the concept of life purpose expanded.

The belief of reincarnation encompasses the possibility that we make choices before each lifetime to learn soul lessons needed on our soul's path. We make contracts with our soul groups, angels and Spirit Guides to accept experiences where we, and the people with whom we will be sharing our lives, have opportunities to learn these needed life lessons. Believing that the choice was mine, even before my birth, gave me comfort.

As my journaling about the purpose of polio and other devastating diseases continued, I delved into a new arena, one that I had never thought about previously. One day, my pen flowed with new questions – why did polio strike this country so hard in the 1940s and 1950s? Was there a lesson for the adults and children of the United States? These polio outbreaks occurred during and after a major world war. Did the brokenness and pain of so many injuries and deaths among our young men release a negative energy that led to the epidemic? Why did so many young children become stricken with this disease? It is ironic that while the television shows in the 1950s often centered around perfect families, with perfect mothers in dresses, high heels, and pearls, there were thousands of families reeling from the effects of polio, whether by untimely deaths or major disabilities. There certainly were many families, and children, who did not look like the idyllic families on television.

One lesson that all of us children stricken with polio may have given the world was a focus on what was really important, and what was not. This country still glorified war and paid little attention to the harm and suffering that millions of people experienced as a result of horrific wars. Soon after the number of polio cases decreased, our country had even more difficult situations – racial strife, three major assassinations, the Vietnam War, the list goes on. It seems our society's priorities continue to be the opposite of the peace and unconditional love the Universe, and our souls, desire.

I also wrote about the life contracts that so many children must have made before we were born into this world. Anyone who knows a polio survivor can verify most of us have certain characteristics. Research shows we are usually Type A personalities. We are highly educated, very successful in our careers, happy in our relationships, and frequently work in the helping professions, often in the medical arena. We are determined, opinionated, and passionate people. We look for the meaning in everyday events in our lives, as well as the meaning of major events. We know suffering, and we work to prevent, or ameliorate it, for others.

A new belief was formulating within me – my personal healing will have effects on many people, and these healings will not be just for my own personal gain. There will be a ripple effect, and it is connected to the healing of other people and the earth. As each person heals, the positive energy of that healing affects others. Eventually, as greater numbers of people heal, the earth too will heal. Finally, as the earth is on the brink of destruction, there seems to be a worldwide recognition of the necessity of healing the earth, including the environment, people, plants and animals. There is a new awareness that everything each of us does has an effect on the whole. In the same way, my healing will contribute a small positive ripple towards the healing of the whole.

There has always been a secret desire in me to write a book.

After all, I love to read and I love books – so why not create one? Could my life purpose be (as I now have been told twice) to share my healing with others, so that other people can heal? And for my fellow polio survivors, can we look at our collective strength and, as a group, forge new territory? While many of us struggle with the effects of post-polio syndrome, is there yet another opportunity for us to teach others?

This journaling work was often eye-opening, inspiring and fun. At other times, it was hard and discouraging. It became a commitment for me, as I had to conscientiously make the time and expend energy to write at a deeper level on a regular basis. I became aware that the process of writing a journal and eventually a book would play a major role in my healing. In fact, I discovered the healing of my emotional self would not be possible without this writing.

I accepted the responsibility for creating my own healing. I could not wish for it, and it would simply happen. I could not search for the right doctor, the right therapy, or the right pill – those things did not exist. There was nothing to be gained from searching outside of my being, as external people and things could not create my healing. Other people could support my healing, but not create my healing. A healing would be a result of working from the inside out – and, the "inside" included emotions, beliefs and thoughts.

My main responsibility was staying connected to God, the Divine, and spiritual guidance would be given to me, at exactly the right pace, at exactly the right time. God is always there for us, but we need to play our part. He places people and opportunities on our life paths. We simply have to say "yes" and participate when these gifts are given to us. He lives in our midst, but we so often ignore the Presence of Spirit in our lives. We simply need to wake up, to become aware of Spirit. Most of all, we have to take ownership for our own growth. Spirit will not do it for us. Miracles do not happen when God waves a magic wand over us

– miracles happen when we participate with His plan. This is living responsibly – God does His part, and we have to do ours.

The opposite of living responsibly is living a passive, victim-like life, waiting for things to get better, but not taking any steps to improve our lives. When we are given thoughts and ideas and experiences, we often choose to ignore them. Or, we choose to procrastinate and make excuses – "this is not the right time"; "it won't work anyway"; "I don't have time to try something new", the list goes on.

It is our decision to take an active role in our personal, spiritual growth and healing, and live a gifted life. Or we can choose to ignore responsible living and live a life of passivity, working against rich possibilities.

Living responsibly requires the willingness to explore the Divine Plan, the openness to accept it, and the courage to live it. It requires action and cooperation on our parts. Sitting back and expecting the Universe to shower us with wonderful gifts simply does not work!

Lesson #13: We must be responsible, active participants to create purposeful lives.

CHAPTER 14

LIVING IN ABUNDANCE

Another gift from my first session with Starr was a book she happened to mention, as she thought it may be helpful to Gary and me. (Or was the "mentioning" of this book another necessary step of Gary's and my spiritual journey?) The book is Paula Horan's *Reiki for Abundance*, and it introduces a Reiki meditative and journaling practice. This book guides the reader, someone who is familiar with Reiki, through a 42-day practice focusing on abundance and lack.

When we think of abundance in our lives, we often think of material possessions. If a person has a big house, a luxurious car, and lots of money in the bank, then it seems he has abundant wealth. If someone does not have these material things, he lacks worldly goods. This book considers abundance vs. lack in broader terms. The timing of the 42-day practice seemed right to us. Both of us had fears about our financial security, as Gary was ending a financially lucrative career and opening a new business just as the recession was in its first days. It seemed doing these meditations could be helpful to us.

Every day there is a brief reading, followed with questions for meditation and journaling. During the meditation time, Reiki is used on yourself to facilitate openness and peacefulness as a response to any new insights. Gary and I did this practice together for 42 consecutive days. While my initial motivation was to find calmness regarding our financial situation, I soon realized there were messages for me regarding the possibility of more healing. For most of my adult life, I never considered the possibility of "getting better." The polio survivors had been told, and I had believed, that we had lived our best days physically. Our best hope was to maintain the physical abilities we had, and many of us were living in a downward spiral, headed towards even greater physical limitations. My attitude was certainly an example of living in the attitude of lack.

This attitude had been gradually changing, though. Reiki, yoga and two healing sessions (with Angela and Starr) had begun to change my old limiting thought patterns. Recently, more emotional healing had occurred through journaling and spending time with my new CD of African drumming and chanting music. These sessions were wonderfully relaxing and healing to my body and spirit.

Day 24 of the Reiki for Abundance exercise dealt with the concept of desire. The reading stated desire is neither good nor bad, but gave reasons why desire is planted in our hearts. Desire can be helpful during our lives when it assists us in finding our life purpose. For example, desire needs to be strong if we approach a challenging career requiring many years of education and study, such as becoming a doctor. Likewise, desire needs to be strong when we make lifelong commitments to another person.

However, desire can also lead us astray if we do not use it towards finding our life purpose and living our spiritual paths. If the only reason for becoming a doctor is to become wealthy, the desire is not in accordance with living out one's life purpose, in a spiritual sense. Desire is healthy and good when it is in alignment with God's plan for us. His plan always serves an important and needed function and serves, in some way, towards the growth of His people.

Healthy desire requires acknowledgement, serious consideration, and then detachment. We need to discern our desires and state them in clear terms. Then, we need to detach ourselves from the results, not judging what happens next. It is very challenging to state our desires to the Universe, and trust the "right" results will occur. It is not easy to fully feel and state the desire, and then become emotionally detached to the final outcomes. Spirit is truly part of the process, and trust and faith is needed to accept the results. If the desire truly fulfills one's life purpose, and one takes appropriate actions to fulfill the desire, Spirit will bless that person with fulfillment of the desire. If one states the desire, but it does not serve one's life purpose, the result is the correct one, whether or not it is the expected result. In other words, one must become detached from the results, and know that the desire was good and right, but it served another purpose.

This concept was somewhat new, and yet somewhat similar, to what I had always believed. I had been taught all prayers are answered, although perhaps not in the way we had wanted, because God knew what was best for us. This new slant challenged me to look at my desires, over my lifetime, regarding a physical cure. During my childhood, the desire to be like other children was strong. I wanted it so bad I could taste it! As I grew older, I viewed those thoughts as childish and self-defeating. I was only making myself upset and not accomplishing anything.

In my case, the desire for a physical cure had been shelved for many years. The desire became an emotion I did not allow myself to feel, and I had disconnected myself from that emotion altogether. Letting go of all desire made it easier to come to a level of acceptance, and I had lived in the acceptance mode for a long time.

Now, the challenge was to allow myself to feel the desire again, without becoming attached to the outcome. That is a very difficult balance, especially with having the history that I'd had with it. I bounced back and forth. Do I even dare to permit myself to feel those feelings again, only to have to detach from them, sooner rather than later? Will I have to experience the pain, all over again, of wanting something so bad I can taste it, and then being devastated when there are no physical improvements? I realized it was important to feel the desire fully again, but to approach it differently this time.

First of all, I now had the belief that anything is possible, and there are no limitations to what Divine Source, with my cooperation, could do. I had to reconnect with my feelings of desire, as being disconnected from my emotions would not lead me to my life purpose. Then, when the reconnection occurred, I had to truly detach from the results, whatever they may be. It seemed paradoxical – to get reconnected, only to detach – and yet I knew I had to live through that process again, in order to fully experience my life purpose. I realized the only way to find any emotional and spiritual healing would be through this process of reconnection and detachment. Whether or not any physical healing occurred would be dependent on what my life purpose truly is. I knew I needed to trust that belief fully, to reach the full potential of my healing.

And I knew trust needed to be a major factor in my healing. Could I build up enough trust to believe that a miracle is possible in my life? Do I think I am worthy of a miracle? The one reality of journaling is that the more you journal, the more questions you develop! Journaling continues to take you to deeper and deeper levels of understanding, and challenge, and growth, if you can find the courage to explore.

Within the first few days of our Reiki for Abundance meditation practice, I also realized how my upbringing affected my feelings of lack. We did not have a lot of material possessions, being such a large family with two adults and nine children, living on a farm. All our relatives and neighbors had to work hard just to make enough money to survive. It seemed everyone worried about the crops and the weather, and life was hard. The feelings of lack and deprivation extended well into my adult years, although these feelings did not match the reality of our middle-class incomes. I started to change this perception and became more grateful for the blessings of our abundant life, financial and otherwise. I started to realize that if Gary's second career was part of his life purpose (and I truly believed it was), we would be blessed with abundance. I needed to quit worrying about the money.

I also realized how these feelings of lack had extended to my perspective of my physical body. There are many things I cannot physically do. I did not view myself as a healthy person, even though I eat healthy foods and take good care of my body.

My journaling focused on my feelings of lack surrounding my health. And, I realized how these feelings did not match the reality. In many areas, my health is excellent for my age. I have excellent blood pressure and cholesterol numbers. My calcium level is high, except for one small area, and that is being addressed. The real problem was my perception of my health. I started to think of myself as a healthy person, and I actually started to feel healthier and stronger. The abundance of good health was always there. What was lacking was my not recognizing it, and not expressing my appreciation of this gift.

Abundance is a state of mind, created by our own thoughts and perceptions. If I view my life as being rich, I am rich – whether it is basked in loving relationships, spiritual connectedness, health, the arts and, perhaps, even money. If I view my life as lacking, all the riches in the world and all the blessings a person can have will still not be enough. All of us are familiar with celebrities and billionaires who still feel empty, because they continue to live within the perception of lack, as they think they do not have enough. And all of us know people with few material possessions who are truly joyful and peaceful. All of us can choose to be grateful for the blessings we have been given and live happily in abundance. Or we can choose to live in lack. It is that simple.

Lesson #14: We choose to live in abundance, or lack.

CHAPTER 15

LIVING IN RHYTHM

I scheduled my second session with Starr just a few weeks later, as I could not wait to see what would happen next. I had been journaling and expanding my beliefs of what healing may be occurring for me, as well as for others on earth. Starr asked me if I had a particular focus, or question, for Spirit. I stated I continued to be concerned about the low calcium level in my left hip, but was also open to any message I needed to receive.

Starr started the session by asking Spirit about my left hip. She was guided to have me lay down on the massage table in the room and to place her hands on my left hip. What she saw in the Spirit World was a little baby girl being removed from the hip by a Spirit. Another figure, who seemed to be a male, appeared. He wore a hooded robe, and Starr could not see his face. He lovingly took the baby from the Spirit, stating he was very sorry for his lack of attention to her. He exuded a sense of shame about his actions, telling Starr he did the best he could at the time. He held the baby with love and walked off with her. Then Mother Mary came, held her healing hands over my hip, and then covered it with a healing salve. She gave Starr instructions that I needed to give the hip time to heal. It would be helpful for me to send Reiki energy to the hip, although not intensely for the first day or two.

Starr and I spent a good amount of time discussing what had happened. There are shamans who do "psychic surgery," which refers to a procedure where skin is actually cut and organs repaired or removed, with no surgical instruments used. That is not what happened to me. My surgery occurred in Spirit World only, and there were no marks on my physical body. However, to my surprise, I had some mild aches in that hip for the next few days. I did not willfully manifest those aches, as I did not expect anything like that to happen. And the aches were not typical and were a different sensation from anything I had ever felt.

Starr wondered if something had happened in this lifetime, such as my losing a child. Although I had experienced a miscarriage, this did not seem to be the right meaning to either of us. I told her about the death of my baby sister Patty, but that possibility did not resonate with us either. Another interpretation Starr suggested was that perhaps something had happened in a previous family generation, and I had carried that sorrow into this lifetime. Or, perhaps something had occurred in a previous life of mine, and I continued to carry that sorrow within me. It seemed to Starr there was a connection to an actual occurrence, rather than a symbolic message. The supposition that I had been carrying a very old sorrow resonated with both of us.

I was quickly learning that if a supposition did not resonate within my heart, it probably was not true. In this scenario, what rang true was that there were old sorrows within me. I have always had periods of sadness that seemed to have no explanation or a connection to anything that was occurring in my life at the time.

During our discussion, I also informed Starr about our work with the *Reiki of Abundance* book. I mentioned some of my journaling was debating the question of emotional or spiritual healing vs. a physical cure, and the role of my desires in exploring those questions. This concept seemed confusing at times. It seemed most of my childhood daydreaming focused on a physical cure, a type of magical thinking common to children. I'd daydream the next morning I'd wake up and walk normally, with no braces or crutches. I'd pray and pray that God would take this affliction away from me. So considering a physical cure at my age seemed childish. It seemed ridiculous to think something would change now, at my age, in my mid-fifties. And I was fearful I would set myself up for a huge letdown. I did not want to go through that kind of pain again. It was easier to stay at the level of acceptance I had so carefully crafted over the years.

On the other hand, a physical cure would be wonderful. I imagined that if a healing occurred, I would greatly rejoice at everything I'd be able to do for the first time in my life – take long walks with my husband, play golf and tennis, run – the activities most people take for granted. A cure for my own enjoyment seemed egotistical and selfish. However, if there was a greater purpose – such as teaching others that healing oneself through spiritual knowledge and interaction was possible – then it would be a truly awesome experience. Moreover, what is wrong with wanting to have the physical abilities that most people have? Back and forth I went, trying to find the right solution.

Starr's initial reaction to my explanation was almost defensive, stating that healing may or may not include a physical cure, and I should not be placing my hopes on that. Then she realized she was reacting judgmentally, involving her own ego and fears in the process, and that was not appropriate either.

So she went to Spirit World with the question of a physical cure vs. an emotional healing for me. She was told that physical healing is part of the plan for my life, although the extent of the healing was not defined. We talked about manifestation and how physical cures and improvements can be manifested. The Universe does not have limits on what is possible; it is only our rational-thinking, human minds that limit Universal possibilities.

We talked about how physical illnesses can be a result of emotional turmoil, either from the current life, a past life, or ancestral memories. We talked about the possibility the polio has served all the purpose it can, up to this point in my life. And now the greater purpose may be served through a physical cure. She asked for another affirmation from Spirit, closed her eyes, and saw Gary and me dancing gracefully across a dance floor. That image was an affirmation for both of us that physical improvements were possible.

This session was certainly more intense than I ever imagined such a session could be. I was learning Spirit World can present Itself in many different ways, and my sessions would be totally unpredictable.

And yet there was a certain rhythm to what I was experiencing. I would feel myself being strongly connected to Spirit, and then I would feel myself backing away from the experience, as if it was too hot to touch. I felt strong belief, and then I felt strong doubt – "Spirit is blessing me with these visions and statements," would be followed with a thought like, "Is this all make-believe?" Faith flowed in, faith flowed out.

All of us live within the rhythms of belief and doubt all the time, but experiences like these bring these rhythms into our conscious awareness. The physical world around us demonstrates rhythms to perfection – the waves and tides of the ocean, the rising and setting of the sun, the seasonal changes demonstrating spring's new growth and autumn's death of the greenery around us. Within our own lives, we experience the ups and downs of mood swings, feeling energetic and then fatigued, and being young and growing old, leading to the deaths of our physical bodies. The rhythm of life is also captured in one of my favorite Bible passages. This familiar verse is from Ecclesiastes, Chapter 3, verses 1-8:

There is an appointed time for everything,
and a time for every affair under the heavens.
A time to be born, and a time to die;
A time to plant, and a time to uproot the plant.
A time to kill, and a time to heal;
A time to tear down, and a time to build;
A time to weep, and a time to laugh;
A time to mourn, and a time to dance.
A time to scatter stones, and a time to gather them;

A time to embrace, and a time to be far from embraces.
A time to seek, and a time to lose;
A time to keep, and a time to cast away.
A time to rend, and a time to sew;
A time to be silent, and a time to speak.
A time to love, and a time to hate;
A time of war, and a time of peace.

Maybe these verses always resonated with me because I related so well to the rhythms of faith in my own life. When we examine our lives, we remember the various periods we have already lived through – up and down, good and bad, love and hate.

All these spiritual concepts are intertwined and one cannot stand alone. Becoming aware of these realities and choosing to live a Spirit-filled life is not an easy journey. Not living in Spirit, though, is an even more difficult journey, as the lack of awareness can lead to a life of despair and sadness, especially during times of darkness. Hope is found when faith is lived to the fullest.

Lesson #15: We can choose to live in rhythm with the Universe.

CHAPTER 16

MORE AFFIRMATIONS!

When one sets the intention to listen to Spirit, wonderful things happen. Everything comes together in a spectacular ways. I had just completed my first two shamanic sessions, and set aside my journaling and meditation for a fun weekend with my sisters.

DOGfest '07 was scheduled during the Apple Festival in northern Indiana. DOGfest is an acronym for Daughters of Ginge (our Mom's nickname), and it is an annual, fun-filled weekend with my four sisters. It is a special bonding time for the five of us, as we laugh, sightsee, shop, eat, and talk, talk, talk. No husbands or children are invited to attend. One of our weekend rituals is to save our birthday gifts for each other throughout the year and open all of them during our special weekend together.

Although part of me wanted to share my experience of the intuitive shamanic sessions with my sisters, I had decided I was not yet ready to share that information. How would I explain it? How exactly was I being healed – was it physical, emotional, and/or spiritual? I thought I should tell my adult children first, and I did not know how or when I'd be comfortable in doing that either. The reality was that I was not comfortable in sharing this information with anyone else yet, except my husband. It would be months before I came to grips with that aspect of my journey.

The gift opening began, and we ooh'd and aah'd at each sister's special selection for another sister. My youngest sister handed me a beautifully wrapped box. When I opened it, I was stunned beyond words, totally speechless. I did not know whether to cry, laugh, or stop breathing – and I think I initially landed in a place of semi-shock for several long minutes. My four sisters stared at me, not knowing what to say or do. Finally I started to sob, and I sobbed uncontrollably for a few minutes, but I was able to spit out that it was all good.

This was the gift that stunned me, to the core of my being. In the box was a Willow Tree angel, the brown, wood-carved angels sold in many gift shops. This angel's head was tilted to the left, and she had a pink conch shell in her left hand, holding it to her left ear, in the exact same way that I was instructed to hold my conch shell to my ear, when I needed guidance for my writing. Since my first session with Starr, I had started every writing session holding my shell to my ear in the exact same position, creating sacred space and asking for guidance.

Could it be any clearer that Spirit is with me and guiding me every step of the way? I knew my second item for my writing time had just been revealed to me, in this very dramatic way. This was more than a synchronicity to me. It was an affirmation, beyond ALL AFFIRMATIONS!!

Eventually, I gained control of myself and took several deep breaths. The explanation I gave to my sisters was a bare-bones sketch of what was occurring. I told them I was seeing a different kind of healer, and my healing process was continuing. They, of course, knew how Reiki had been alleviating my fatigue. I stated that, although in many ways over the years I had adjusted well to the polio and every way it had affected me, there were still deeper levels of emotions in need of further healing.

I continued by telling them the healer was intuitive and had received messages from an angel, for me. I had been given directions, through the angel, to do frequent journaling, and she would guide me through the journaling process. (I knew an angel would be more acceptable to them, than saying I was seeing a shamanic healer who visited the Spirit World.) I also shared I had been given directions to choose one of the shells in my house to have with me during this writing time, and how I had held the shell to my ear before writing. And, I was told another item would be revealed to me soon. I knew this angel was the second item.

I also told them to keep this a secret for now, as I had not yet told my children, and I was not ready to share it with other people at all. All of them thought it was really neat! They supported me in my efforts to seek more healing, and they truly appreciated the synchronicities in my story.

I was aware this story was not exactly the whole truth, but rather a sanitized and shortened version. I was aware of my own lack of readiness in sharing my journey with others and knew at some point, I'd have to come to terms with this reality, if I was to write and publish a book!

After the weekend, my journaling took on a special quality. I strongly felt the presence of Spirit every time I wrote. For several weeks, the third item eluded me. Finally, one morning, when I awoke long before the alarm clock radio played its wake-up music, I remembered a particular item. It was a crystal. I got out of bed and walked over to the bookcase in our bedroom. I found the small box where the crystal was stored, held it, and thanked my Spirit Guide for reminding me of this gift. After further meditation, I knew the crystal was my third item.

This crystal had been given to me several years earlier in Pittsburgh by a person who told me she had been guided to buy it for me. Unfortunately, this relationship did not end on a positive note, and I'd had mixed feelings about keeping the crystal. On one hand, it seemed that if Spirit wanted me to have the crystal, I should keep it. On the other hand, every time I looked at it, negative feelings filled my heart. I discussed my dilemma with a friend who knew a psychic, and she took it to him, with the simple question – Should her friend keep this crystal, or not? He told her this crystal was meant to be kept by me, but it was covered with negative residue. My friend explained my dilemma to him, and he instructed her on how to cleanse the crystal of the negative energies.

The psychic related what he saw, with the crystal. He saw a

medicine man associated with the crystal who wanted to work with me and bring me further healing. He described the medicine man as dark-skinned, with long hair, in a long robe, perhaps from South America or Africa. In Pittsburgh, I occasionally held the crystal in my hands during meditation, and asked the medicine man to direct his positive energy to me. It was a pleasant experience, but I did not have especially strong feelings about the crystal. After our move to Asheville, I had not used it at all and had almost forgotten about it. That morning, I was reminded to find the crystal again.

African tribe, medicine man – finally, it struck me! The medicine man is part of the tribe that appeared to Starr during my first shamanic session. My third item had been with me all along, but my lack of awareness had prevented me from remembering the gifts I had already received. I also remembered, at that moment, the message from my first session with Starr – many things had already occurred in my life to lead me to a more complete healing. I remembered the direction to "remember" from the first session. I felt overwhelming gratitude for the revelation of all three items.

Everything happens for a reason. I was blessed with a beautiful gift from my sister, a gift I will always, always cherish. Whenever I feel doubt, all I have to do is hold the carved angel, with the shell held to her ear, and remember how stunned I was when I opened the gift. Whenever I wonder about the difficulties in life, all I have to do is remember the gift of the crystal – even though it was from a person with whom I no longer have a relationship. We learn lessons in strange and wonderful ways. The message was clear to me. As I become more open to the messages of Spirit, there will be no end to small miracles.

Lesson #16: God graces us with affirmations when we live in alignment with Spirit.

CHAPTER 17

PROCESSING IT ALL

I could barely contain my excitement! I could not wait to show Starr my angel figurine holding the conch shell to her ear, and tell her the third item had also been revealed to me. She was quite amazed by the angel! She quickly connected with the Spirit World, and she was told yes, Spirit had inspired my sister to buy the angel for me several months earlier. Spirit said my sister bought it before I had even met Starr. The angel was a sign from Spirit I was on the right path. Also, Starr was told I do have a "Writing Angel," the Spirit providing guidance and direction during my writing time.

We were also reminded my healing process has been in place for some time, and many things had already occurred in my life to give me healing. I felt the truth in that statement, as I recalled how Reiki, Angela's healing session, yoga, the sessions with Valerie, and other occurrences had already brought me healing. I knew I was moving forward, just as I was meant to be.

(After this session, I called my youngest sister to thank her again for the gift and ask what inspired her to buy the angel for me. She stated she was browsing through a catalog earlier in the summer, saw the angel, and thought I'd like it for my birthday gift – as simple as that. Inspiration is often this simple.)

I also shared with Starr my feelings of being hesitant to tell my family and friends about these sessions. I told her how I had to give my sisters a little information, due to my reaction to the gift, but I was not yet ready to tell my children. I said one reason for not telling my children was that my daughter was getting married the following summer, and I did not want to "rain on her parade" with my own excitement of a possible physical cure.

Starr looked at me quizzically, stating this reason did not resonate with her. She thought perhaps the real reason had to do with my fears. Immediately, I knew she was right, but could not admit to it yet, out loud. What I did say was that I would journal on that thought and try to come up with what was underneath my reluctance. Oooh, sometimes it is hard to acknowledge the truth within our hearts.

Starr entered the Spirit World again. She and I were among the African tribe. There was great joy and dancing among the tribal members again when they saw me. I was in the center of a tribal dancing circle, and the dancing and music was contributing to my healing. As Starr related this scene to me, I started thinking about whether or not a physical cure would occur, and if I would attain full, normal use of my legs.

Later, when Starr returned to the Spirit World, the leader looked at me with some dismay, stating I am worrying too much, and there is nothing to worry about, as my healing has been in process for a long time. I simply needed to trust all the guidance given to me thus far, and the guidance that was still coming to me, through my journaling and writing. He stated, several times, all I needed to do was – remember. Remember, remember, and I would move forward. He did not tell Starr exactly what I needed to remember - memories from this lifetime, a previous lifetime, spiritual inspirations, or what - but memories would also play a role in my healing.

As we left the dancing circle, I walked, without a limp, next to Starr. She received a message I had lived in the ocean a long, long time ago. She also talked about the significance of water and sunlight to me in this lifetime. That statement strongly resonated with me!

Overall, this session gave me reassurance and affirmation that I am on the right path. I would ask for memory recall when I wrote.

What fun it was to journal on water and sunlight! I wrote

about the significance of water and sunlight in my life. I always loved playing in the water. As a little girl, I have fond memories of my family visiting a great aunt and uncle at their lake cottage every summer. I was always able to move my legs easily in the warm, buoyant lake water. During those long, hot afternoons, I felt "normal," as it seemed I could move and swim just like other children could.

During my adult years, I developed a great fondness for the ocean and beautiful sandy beaches. My first trip to an ocean beach was our honeymoon to the Caribbean, in the middle of January, after a very cold wedding day in Indiana. It felt like we were plucked out of a frozen zone and plopped into a paradise. Beautiful palm trees, sparkling white sand, and crystal-clear blue, warm water – what a lovely way to start our married lives together! I always loved our subsequent vacations to beaches, and I had loved living in Rhode Island where we could jump in the car and be on a sandy beach within an hour. Thinking about spending an afternoon on a sandy beach causes my soul to smile. There is no more peaceful place on earth, even if I am surrounded by chatty people on blankets and blaring loud music. My soul feels the never-ending love of God at a beach. For me, watching or playing in the ocean waves is heaven on earth.

And my faith tradition also embraces many meanings for water. There is the water of Baptism, a symbol of new spiritual life. Holy water is used on special occasions and holy days to bless us with God's abundance. There is a wonderful flow to water which can be compared to the Divine Flow of Love.

Proximity to the beaches, the beauty of the mountains, and sunlight contributed to our reasons to move to Asheville, North Carolina. It is a rare day when the sun does not shine in Asheville, as compared to Pittsburgh, where day after day of sobering gray clouds is not unusual. I wanted to live in sunshine, as I always feel more energetic and happy when days are filled with warm, yellow light. I wanted a house with many windows and natural light, and that is exactly what we found. I became more aware of the connection between our desire to live in North Carolina and my life purpose to become healed. I approached each journaling episode with joy. It was simply fun to ponder all these lovely memories.

Then, "normal life" took over for the next few months. We made several trips to visit family over the holidays; major changes at my workplace occurred; decisions around house improvements were made; efforts to build the massage therapy business continued. Life was simply busy. Journaling became more sporadic. It became a second priority in my life, after everything else. I was beginning to lose momentum.

Sometimes, my mind would question if all this was real. Then I would look at my angel holding the shell, the chosen conch shell, and my crystal and know it was real. I would remember all the synchronicities and events that brought me to this day, and I would make a new commitment to myself to journal and write more frequently.

One thing I never stopped, though, was my daily Reiki practice. Reiki had become a normal part of my daily routine, not unlike brushing my teeth frequently, or taking a shower. It was a gift I used and greatly appreciated. On a physical level, it kept my energy level high. On an emotional level, it kept me calm, serene, balanced. On a spiritual level, it kept me connected to God, to Spirit. Using Reiki daily is like a form of meditation for me – there are benefits to every aspect of my humanity.

Another phenomenon was occurring too. It seems our human minds cannot absorb and integrate, great amounts of spiritual knowledge at one time. It takes weeks, months, years, a whole lifetime, to process all this information and integrate new beliefs into our old belief systems. Taking that kind of time is an essential ingredient to full integration. It is not possible to learn new information and change our belief systems overnight. It requires exploring, experimenting, and integrating all this new information into our lives, day to day. It is truly a process. Just like a wedding day does not make a marriage, singular events (although these events may be spectacular and mind-blowing) do not change one's belief system. It is a process.

When I think about my Catholic faith, I know that eight years of Catholic school, attendance at Sunday Masses with its sermons, discussions with family and friends, and reading were needed to develop a strong foundation. In the same way, integrating these new experiences of visiting the Spirit World and redefining how healing occurs were requirements in developing my expanded belief system. I was not throwing out my old beliefs, but rather I was adding to them and making subtle shifts. In my journaling, and in my mind, I was discerning what is truth, and what is not. I was deciding what to believe, and what not to believe. While I continued to honor and believe many aspects of my Catholic tradition, I no longer limited myself to only that tradition.

After the holidays were over and my enthusiasm for journaling was waning, I knew it was important to recommit to my healing. So I made an appointment with Starr to have another shamanic healing session. Participating in shamanic healing sessions was part of the process of healing my body, emotions and spirit – but the sessions were just one part of the process. It was necessary for me to further explore what I learned during each session, redefine my beliefs, and integrate everything into my whole being. It truly is a lifelong process.

Lesson #17: Spiritual growth creates integrated wholeness.

CHAPTER 18

MANIFESTATION

I felt, to the core of my being, that I was living on the right path of healing. I entered my next shamanic healing session with total openness to any guidance that would come that day. I told Starr it seemed I needed to have some time off between sessions, but it was now time to focus on further healing.

Starr totally accepted my listening to my own intuition to guide me along my path, deciding my next steps. Starr went to Spirit World and reported the African tribe appeared immediately and instructed her to have me lay on the massage table. She was instructed to lay her hands on my right leg, one on the knee and the other on my ankle. She spent quite a while on that position while I relaxed and felt the warmth coming through her hands, similar to a Reiki treatment.

When she was finished, she told me further healing had occurred and explained what had happened. She and I were in the Spirit World, and the African tribe conducted a healing ceremony on me. There was a crystal lying across my stomach, and she described perfectly the color and shape of the crystal from Pittsburgh, the crystal that was the third revealed item for my writing time. (Prior to this session, I had often been guided to lay the crystal across my stomach at home during Reiki treatments.) One tribesman stood over me during this treatment, while the other members sang and danced.

I believe the tribesman is the medicine man associated with this crystal, the medicine man seen by the Pittsburgh psychic. My healing tools have a way of being reintegrated time and again in my healing process. I also experience these references as affirmations that I am on the correct path.

Then several of the tribesmen stood at my right foot and pulled a large piece of brown-colored sludge through the bottom of my foot. Starr explained the sludge was about as long as my right leg, and it was time for it to be removed from my body, where it had lived many years. The tribesmen handed it to her to dispose of it. There was some resistance from the sludge to leave me, but Starr gently told it I would be fine without it. She and the others thanked the sludge for serving its purpose in my life, but it needed to leave me now. She continued to express loving gratitude towards it.

The leader of the tribe stepped forward and stated it was time for the sludge to go into water, and magically a body of water appeared behind Starr. She noted it felt incongruent to have this water in the jungle environment, but there it was. She walked over to the water and gently placed the sludge into it. While it dissipated into many pieces, she continued to thank and reassure it that it now belonged in the water, and I would be fine without it.

Starr and I discussed what this sludge represented, in my life. While we had no definitive answers to this question, we agreed that it could be negative energies from the polio, or other negative thoughts, or events in my life, past lives, or ancestral problems. I was learning that our energies can take on human characteristics and have a life and personality of their own. Our energies are alive, with their own emotions, and energies are affected by our personal emotions. This brown sludge was alive and real, it had been attached to me for many years, and it did not want to leave. It took Starr sending it gratitude and reassurance for its agreement to finally leave my being.

During our discussion, I made a comment to Starr how pleased and grateful I am to have her be a part of my journey, and bringing the healing African tribe to me. She quickly corrected me, stating I had access to the tribe whenever I wanted, that I could call upon them anytime to hasten my healing, and my healing was not dependent upon having sessions with her. I knew that was true, as often I felt a presence of Spirit around me, while I listened to the African music CD and meditated, often with the crystal lying across my stomach, and warm healing energies coming from my hands. At the same time, I knew these intuitive shamanic sessions were helpful, bringing deeper levels of understanding and knowledge to me. This cast of characters represented parts of me – I could call on these energies to bring forth my healing.

I realized that I had choices to make. I could participate actively in my healing by connecting with Spirit World. Or, I could choose not to utilize these Spirits, and stay where I had lived for so many years.

That was no longer a choice for me. I now believed that I could manifest a healing, whether it be physical, emotional, and/or spiritual, to my being. If I simply changed my emotions, thoughts, and beliefs, anything was possible. I could manifest anything, if I truly believed it was possible.

The possibilities of manifestation became even more real to me during the next session. The title of my story, "Believe and It Is True" was given to me during that healing session. Both Starr and I are white American women who lived within the confines of traditional belief systems during our childhoods, and for most of our adult years. And yet, here we were, in a small therapy room in an old, large house in Asheville, communicating with the Spirit World! Today's session was different than previous ones I'd had with Starr. The drama seemed less intense, but the messages were just as powerful.

This time, I arrived with a burning question for Spirit. It seemed I had hit a plateau with my healing, and I was wondering if I should be doing more things, or seeing an additional healer. I had looked on the Internet for African drumming healers, and I also was considering scheduling an appointment with the first healing person I had visited in

Pittsburgh. My question was whether or not I was supposed to seek another healer. Was Starr simply one of a larger group of healers that I needed? Was she the only person I needed to see now? Am I on the right path to healing? It is never easy to get rid of the doubts manufactured by our human minds.

The session began with my reporting a few subtle, physical changes that Gary and I noticed recently. My right foot, that had been as flat as a pancake with no arch for as long as I can remember, now had a small arch to it. When I stand on it, it no longer turns inward as far as it had. I continue to notice that my spine and back feel straighter when I walk. And the calves on both legs are growing thicker, with muscles developing in more pronounced ways. These changes seemed minimal, and yet significant, at the same time. The minimal part is that the changes occurred in a slow and subtle pace. These changes are not noticeable to other people. At the same time, even subtle changes are significant, as there had been no changes for the past five decades of my life. Changes like these had never happened to me before!

During today's session, a spirit medicine worked with us. This Spirit guided us to journey into a jungle in Spirit World. Once again, I was asked to lie down on the massage table.

My time on the table was brief, as compared to the last session. Starr was instructed to lay her hands on my right leg, left hand on the knee and right hand on the ankle. After a few minutes, she moved her left hand to my right hip. Her hands became very warm, again feeling like the warm, soothing energy of Reiki. One of the first messages she received was that Gary needs to practice a kind of massage-stretching-water therapy on me. And I was to be the first person on whom he'd practice this method.

Gary had also had a session with Starr a few months earlier, where the main focus was his transition from being an engineer to becoming a massage therapist. In that session, a Spirit Guide had stated that he was to explore the possibility of doing massage in water. He had not yet looked into that arena to see if any methods like this existed. This was the second time this message was given to us.

Starr reported when she asked Spirit my question about contacting other healers for further healing, Spirit replied, "What about the book?" I felt chagrined immediately, for I knew writing the book had slipped to the backburner of my busy life over the past several months. While I continued to journal, somewhat sporadically I must admit, I had actually only sat down at the computer two times to begin writing a manuscript. Only six pages were typed! The Spirit explained I had everything I needed to be healed – writing the book is part of the healing process itself. The process of journaling and writing would be an essential part of the process of healing. Finally, I understood.

Starr's and my discussion that occurred after the journeying into Spirit World was the most important part of this session for me. We discussed how difficult it is to stay focused on the most essential things in our lives, and how easy it is to do everything else first. I needed to become a "real" writer and dedicate blocks of time, on a regular basis, if I was to ever finish the book – and if I was ever to be healed. I knew this was true, especially in my very full, busy life.

I needed to recommit myself to this healing process, or it would take years and years, or never occur at all. Manifestation of our desires requires commitment and time, and if this is truly what I wanted, then why was I not making time for it? Manifesting a healing requires full cooperation – intention, thought and action. I could not simply desire something, and sit back passively, waiting for it to happen. I needed to be an active participant in the healing and writing processes.

We went back to one of my original dilemmas of last fall – was I to be healed in the emotional and spiritual realms only, or was I to experience a physical healing? We discussed the concept of my self-centered, egotistical desires of wanting to look normal and pretty vs. the altruistic desire to help others by spreading the message of healing to the world. We revisited the concept that it is okay to be excited about the possibility of a physical cure, but not become attached to that outcome. Spirit wants us to be joyful and happy, as long as it brings no harm to ourselves or others.

We discussed my need to claim my power, in the true sense of what power means. In our society, power has so many negative connotations and power is often associated with controlling other people and systems. Often greed and corruption are also connected with the negative use of power.

Legitimate power means to claim our birthright to be whole and perfect. It is that simple. Legitimate power is a possibility for every person, not just for the privileged few. However, "whole and perfect" is not referring to the physical body, especially as that is defined by our current American culture. "Whole and perfect" refers to the beauty of all God's creations on this earth. His divine unconditional love is what creates that whole-ness and perfection.

I needed to believe – one hundred percent – that I am whole and perfect, even in a body with physical imperfections. But I also needed to believe it was possible to heal the physical imper-fections and have a normally functioning body. I needed to understand my physical state does not determine my wholeness and perfection. Accepting the concept of wholeness and perfection is an acknowledgement that God creates us in perfection. It is a total belief in the fact that all of us are Divine creatures and are perfect in the eyes of God. Only our own faulty perceptions prevent us from accepting ourselves as being less than Divine. When my focus is on healing my mind and spirit to accept the reality that I am already perfect, then a physical healing is possible. The only thing stopping me from a physical cure was my old belief.

Starr shared that when her hands were placed on my right leg and foot, she heard Spirit repeat over and over, "Believe and it is true. Believe and it is true. Believe and it is true." Then Starr saw me walking towards her normally, with no limp at all. I had on a business suit with a short skirt, wearing high heels. At first, I had on stiletto heels. Starr said to the Spirit, "No, no, the heels need to be age-appropriate," and the shoes changed to lower-heeled pumps, the kind a middle-aged woman would wear. Who said Spirit does not have a sense of humor?

Starr was also informed that while my beliefs for a physical cure are strong, there are sometimes doubts. I acknowledged the truth of that statement. I also shared with Starr that sometimes I struggle with the traditional Catholic American white woman being healed in such an alternative way, and how would I explain it to family and friends? As soon as I said the words out loud for the first time (they had only been thoughts before), my eyes welled with tears. I said, "My family and friends would be so happy to see me walk normally, they would not care how it happened." And, I knew that statement was the real truth!

We talked about how amazing it was that there was a message for Gary in my session, and how he was part of my healing process. A light bulb went off in my head – Gary is one of my healers! That statement may seem rather ironic, since I have been talking about his doing Reiki and massage for me the past several years. Yet I had not seen him as one of my "healers" – and there is a difference in the two ways of seeing him. I had seen him as providing energy and body work for me, not unlike going to a professional to have those wonderful, energizing things done for you. Here I've been, the past few months, trying to figure out if I was supposed to work with another healer, while living with one of them all along. Sometimes, I'm just dense, and I excel in having lots of "duh" moments! I have this funny image that God has to come down and hit me over the head with a 2" x 4" piece of lumber to get my attention. In other words, He has to send me a message several times before I get it. Unfortunately, isn't that the way it is for most of us?

Most importantly, however, the other inspiration I had that day was the recognition that true healing begins with me – and only me. I know now, without a doubt, that I have the capacity to heal myself. No doubts, no worries, no ifs, ands or buts about it. I have everything I need, confirmed by the words of this wonderful Spirit medicine. I do not need to keep seeking new and different kinds of healers. I simply need to believe in, and work with, God's healing powers that are available to me.

I left the session with renewed hope and a renewed commitment to refocus on my writing and, ultimately, my healing. This session recharged my batteries and my commitment to heal myself entirely, as much as possible during this lifetime. I suddenly "found" the time to write on the computer, although my busy lifestyle did not slow down at all. Frequently, I set aside hours of time to meditate, journal, and sit at the computer, like scheduling an appointment with myself. I create sacred space by bringing my journal, conch shell, angel and crystal, and setting them on the shelves of our computer armoire. The words flow. More levels of understanding come to me.

I am living out the manifestation of a total healing. No matter what happens to me physically, I am healing. I am healing on many levels – if it is physical and my body looks more "normal," great. If not, that is okay, too – as I am healing myself emotionally and spiritually. I am learning what healing really means. Manifestation can be described by the phrase that was given to me – believe and it is true. So simple and yet so profound.

Lesson #18: True healing begins with me.

CHAPTER 19

FINDING BALANCE

It seems other-world experiences need to be balanced with everyday life-on-earth experiences. And, my life certainly is that! Living my life in the "normal" world of my hospice work, maintaining our home and yard, helping with Gary's business, connecting with family and friends, and of course, reading books, filled my days. But, I also found time to meditate, journal, and type on the computer. Somehow, I'm finding the balance of living on earth and living in alignment with Spirit, going back and forth on a daily basis. In fact, I'm finding the more time I spend with Spirit, the more joy I find in my everyday life on earth.

Another book that Starr recommended I read, *Shaman, Healer, and Sage* by Alberto Villoldo, was one that I greatly enjoyed. I was beginning to understand that shamanic healing has many forms and belief systems, not unlike the more traditional religions that are more familiar to us. Villoldo studied the Peruvian traditions. Several sections spoke to me loudly – the first being the difference between healing vs. curing. I had already done a fair amount of mental wrestling, and journaling on that one, specific question. The second phrase he mentioned (and the phrase was just a mention in the book, not fully developed at all) was that one needed to love her disease in order to heal it. That statement jumped off the page into my heart. I knew I had to explore that concept further.

So I spent a lot of time meditating and journaling on the concept of loving my disease. I realized that I had already lived through two major phases already, in dealing with my polio. The first phase was negative – I despised polio, I wished it had never happened to me, I wanted it to go away, I looked at my legs with disgust and sadness. Then, over the years, I grew into the second phase. I learned to accept my condition and developed a normal, American-style life. However, this level of acceptance resulted in an unhealthy place that I visited briefly in recent years. It needed further exploration. The place was one of disconnectedness – I had disconnected my heart from my physical body. In other words, I cut myself off from my feelings about the polio, and thought little about my legs and feet. These body parts were simply a cross that I had to bear, and I concentrated on the other aspects of my life. I saw my intelligence, my compassion, my therapeutic abilities, and my personality as the "real" me. The polio was not who I really was, at all. I tried to forget that I ever had the disease and tried to see myself as someone without any physical limitations. I saw myself as a good person, with a defect that did not really matter.

Some may view this perspective as being emotionally strong. However, it is never emotionally healthy to be disconnected from a part of yourself. Being fully integrated and balanced is healthy. Disconnnected-ness rises out of hate and fear, while full integration rises from love and total acceptance of ourselves as Divinely-created human beings. As I processed all these thoughts and attitudes, I saw how I needed to reintegrate positive feelings and thoughts into my self-image, if I was to heal. I needed to view myself in a balanced way to define myself in a holistic and healthy way.

The previous session had guided Gary and me in some specific directions to promote physical healing. He started to massage my legs and feet in very warm water. It felt wonderful to have my legs and feet gently stretched, and my gnarled toes tugged in straight directions. While watching TV or reading, I sat and rubbed my feet and legs. I continued to do frequent Reiki on them, knowing that I was healing through touch and healing energy. I was connecting again to my physical self, and that was something I had rarely done previously. It had seemed it was less painful to simply ignore the parts of me I did not like. It felt new, like finding a treasured book that you had read years earlier, and re-reading it, only to rediscover the treasures you had known previously. It was like reconnecting with a long-lost, dear friend. It felt good and right, developing wholeness again. I was a complete person, and the last time I identified myself that way was the time prior to having polio. In other words, viewing myself as a whole person, a complete package, had left my self-image at the age of three years old.

The self-healing aspect was starting to make sense to me. I did not need to run out and find another healer, or continue to depend on someone else in order to find complete healing. It would be the Spirit within me and my trust and belief in the Divine Spirit, God. And we would be using some of the tools that have been gifted to me and Gary over the years. Not to mention, utilizing the people that the Universe put into my life, just at the right time. That would be another important step.

Distrust and doubts that this was really happening also continued during these weeks. Doubts would arise in my mind and I made efforts to chase them away. My human self, my ego, would throw piercing thoughts my way – why would this happen now? Do you really think you have the power to heal yourself? Leave well enough alone – you have a good life, why take the risk? What will people think? How will you explain to your religious friends that you are seeing a shamanic healer? The list went on.

But my spiritual side fought back with positive thoughts and new belief statements. I thanked the Universe for all the many signs and synchronicities that I'd been given. I gazed at my shell, my angel, my crystal, with great gratitude. Then my belief, my knowledge, my wisdom, became strong again, and my conviction to stay the course of my spiritual path strengthened. Striving to live a balanced life assisted me with juggling all these different thoughts and practices. Reintegrating parts of myself that I had cut off so many years ago was the most important lesson during this time. I could not heal if I was not whole. I could not live in the Spirit World exclusively, and I could not live in the physical world exclusively. Balancing all these aspects of my life became an intention, and it became an essential part of the process of my healing.

Lesson #19: Balance is an essential element in creating wholeness.

CHAPTER 20

MAKING CHOICES

About six weeks passed until it felt like the right time to have my next shamanic healing session with Starr. For a few days prior to the appointment, Charles, a Spirit Guide who had revealed himself to me during the psychic development classes several years earlier, popped into my mind several times. I felt the desire to know more about my Spirit Guides, and what their roles were in my healing journey. I wondered if Charles was playing a part, and that was why he came into my thoughts during the week.

I told Starr that was my main question for this session, but, of course, I was open to anything that needed to happen during the session. I told her about Charles who had made himself known to me several years earlier. Starr explained her interpretation of Spirit Guides to me. She believes they are representations, or parts, of our divine True Self, and they will present to us in ways we can understand and accept. There may be a Spirit Guide who is with us our entire lifetime. Or particular Guides may be with us to serve a specific role during a time in our lives and leave when that purpose has been served. Spirit Guides can take on any form, and present as people, animals, or anything that will have meaning to a person.

Much to my surprise, she stated she had felt directed the past few days to have me take a more active role in these sessions. She asked if I had ever journeyed to the Spirit World. I described how Valerie had taught us to imagine a large beam of protective light, then stepping into the beam, and rising up. We would step out of the beam, cross over a rainbow-colored bridge, and walk into a beautiful garden.

Starr agreed a person can use any mechanism that works to

travel to the sacred world of Spirit. The most important aspect is to ask for protection while leaving the physical plane and experiencing the spiritual plane. She liked the method I'd been taught and instructed me to close my eyes and see myself rising up in the beam of light, crossing the bridge, and walking into the garden. She instructed me to ask Charles to join us today, and she would be with us, too.

Initially, I felt resistance to this suggestion. I thought Starr is so gifted and knowledgeable in this area, and I am not. I had doubts anything meaningful would occur. Shortly, I realized the fallacies of these thoughts – any person can believe in Spirit and experience it. And I had already done it, many times. Although the main purpose of Valerie's classes had been psychic development, it was an experience of Spirit, in a slightly different way. Every time I meditate and write, I experience Spirit. Any time I think about Spirit and ask for guidance, I experience Spirit. Prayer is simply talking to Spirit. I had a lifetime of experience!

So I calmed myself and proceeded to utilize the method that Valerie had taught me to visit Spirit World. I set the intention for Charles to join us, by asking him to be with us. I saw him in my mind's eye, as he walked towards me in the garden. He appeared as strong and handsome as ever. Starr offered a few questions that I could ask him, and the replies were thoughts in my mind. He stated one of his purposes is to send me strength, when I need it. He stated he often assists me to find my own strength and power, and he has been working with me closely more recently. Starr saw him gazing at me with pure love, while at the same time, taking out his sword and fighting back negative energy forces trying to infiltrate me. She stated he is a great protector of me, and he loves me totally.

The next hour was spent alternating between the physical world and the Spirit World, and Starr and I sharing verbally what each of us saw and experienced there.

Through Starr's gentle encouragement, I asked Charles why

he is appearing in my life more frequently now. He replied that I needed to feel his strength and love during my healing process, and he merged into my body. Both Starr and I saw his Spirit walk into me, and felt him settling into my heart. I felt my heart expand and grow warm with unconditional love. It was a wonderful feeling! I simply sat and felt it for a while. Yummy.

Verbally, I told Starr about the struggles I had been having with trust and belief, and she normalized these for me, stating that every person goes through hills and valleys of belief. I told her about the time in my childhood when I prayed and prayed, and believed that if I prayed hard enough, that I would wake up one morning, perfectly normal. She said, "you must have been disappointed," and I immediately replied, "no, not disappointed, deeply wounded." Then, the tears flowed.

Starr was guided to ask me to find that little girl again, just like the first session we had had together, months earlier. Since that first session, I had thought about my little-girl self, from time to time. I would imagine her, and tell her how beautiful she is, and how she is loved by me and everyone who knows her.

It was easy to see her again, in my mind's eye. Today, she looked very sad, and she was crying. Starr asked me how little she was, and I replied immediately, "four years old." (I did not even think about the answer, the words just came out of my mouth.) Starr talked about the trauma of polio that I had experienced at that age, and I added, "and my grandpa died too." My paternal grandfather died about six months after I got polio. I suddenly realized that his death must have been very traumatic for me, so soon after the onset of polio. It must have seemed that the secure world I had known was growing quite insecure and crumbling around me.

I asked my little girl self what she needed. Her first response was a hug! So, I imagined myself hugging her, and then Charles came, and put his large, strong arms around both of us. Yummy, again. Then, she wanted kisses, and I happily gave her many kisses. We played together for a few minutes, until she became very happy.

I felt such intense unconditional love from them. Charles took the little girl's hand, and they merged together, walking right into my heart. Again, my heart felt abundant love and warmth, and I sat with these feelings awhile, allowing myself to absorb the loving sensations.

While Starr saw me sitting with those wonderful feelings, Charles also revealed another scene to her that had occurred before my birth. My physical body was being assembled, and Charles was placing different organs into it, with great love. Then, he showed her the act of his placing the polio into my body, again with love. He told Starr the polio had always been a part of my life purpose, and that it is greatly loved by Spirit. I also need to express my love to the polio.

When we returned our attention to the physical world, we shared our spiritual experiences. I told Starr how I'd spent the last six weeks, processing the disconnectedness that I had discovered, between my physical self and my emotional self. I told her about the foot and leg massages that Gary had been doing for me. I told her about loving my disease, and how that was different than the level of acceptance that I had lived in for many years. Now, for the second time in two sessions, I had received the message that I needed to love my polio.

Throughout my explanation, she stopped me a few times, and repeated what I had just said. For example, I stated my level of acceptance was so strong, people had often told me once they got to know me, they almost forgot I even had polio. I said they only saw the good aspects of me and I had always appreciated others' abilities to see beyond the polio. Starr stopped me, stating, "you make it sound like polio is a bad part of you, and it is not bad, it is you." Wow, my words reflect my beliefs, and my belief that I am defective is still alive and well! Years of old thoughts and beliefs are not easy to change. It takes conscious effort to change long-held belief patterns.

Also, she pointed out how frequently I use the phrases, "I have to," "I should," etc. It is true, I am a strong critic of myself and judge my thoughts and feelings harshly. My expectations for myself are unrealistic. I have learned thoughts and emotions create our realities, and having these negative thoughts would impede any healing. I vowed to rid myself of these limiting beliefs, once and for all (knowing that my human self would still easily slip back into old habits).

My level of awareness grew during this session, and I am better equipped to call myself on these negative thoughts. After the session, I asked my husband to call me on it, too, when he hears me making negative comments about myself.

Starr suggested that we ask Charles for specific instructions on what I needed to do to continue my healing. I sat back, closed my eyes, and floated into a mystical experience. I felt totally surrounded by a loving, positive energy. I visualized a bubble around me and felt a Spiritual Presence. It was awesome. When I came back, I told Starr about how wonderful this experience was! However, I had not received any specific instructions from Charles. She laughed, stating she and Charles saw that I was enjoying the pure spiritual energies, so Charles talked to her, giving her specific instructions for me. She commented, "you got the great experience, and I got the instructions."

His first instruction to me was to make loving statements to my body parts. Starr demonstrated, putting both hands on her feet, stating, "I love you, feet." She said I should not qualify the statements in any way, like, "I love you, feet, just the way you are," or anything like that. Just "I love you, legs; I love you, hands; I love you, heart." She said I needed to be "big" and "dramatic" about this, as I had a lot of old tapes in my mind to erase, and re-write. I needed to do it often. I was not to ask for healing, or do Reiki, during these exercises, but simply give love, love, love. No conditions, no strings attached – just pure, unconditional love. This resonated strongly with me, as over the years I have had many negative thoughts about my body. My body parts would need to hear these statements loud and clear, repeatedly, to believe it.

Charles also told her I needed to concentrate on the place in my body where he had placed the polio before my birth. She asked him where in my body that would be, and he replied, "she will know." When she told me this, I knew he was referring to my lower spine. It has been my understanding the polio virus settled in an area of the spine. If the virus settled in higher vertebrae, the lungs or arms may be affected, while a lower location on the spine affected the lower limbs. Many times, I had visualized the polio virus in my lower back. It feels as if I had an emotional memory of a sensation there, when I was three years old, although I have no cognitive memories of feeling any pain when the polio manifested in my body. So, I will make loving statements to my lower spine, too. Charles also instructed me to ponder my own strength and power.

I went home and over the next weeks and months, I simply made loving statements to my affected body parts. That is certainly a counter-cultural exercise. We women especially are taught that perfect bodies look like the touched-up ones on magazine covers. Anything less is not pretty, or lovable. Here I was, being given the task to love the body parts that the world would certainly view as not pretty. This was such a new experience for me, it felt odd at first. But then, I truly had fun doing it!

In my journal, I deeply explored my beliefs about beauty. I wrote about how I had bought into the world's view of beauty and love. I wrote about Christopher Reeves; how he lived his life after his accident and resulting paralysis had touched me deeply. He lived a life of expressing love, even when his body could no longer move. His spirit was stronger than his body, and it is his spirit that we remember now. When his body became paralyzed, his spirit grew larger and larger, and affected literally tens of thousands of people. Before his tragic accident, he was just another successful, handsome actor in the eyes of the world. His true power and life purpose were fully expressed after he became paralyzed. All of us can find a way to express the essences of our souls, if we grow in awareness, and put some time, intention and positive energy into it.

I was exploring a new paradox. And isn't life always full of paradoxes? While I practiced loving my so-called "defective" body parts, I grew in the knowledge of how insignificant having so-called "normal" body parts truly is. If you had made that statement to me several years ago, my intellect may have agreed with you. But it is a whole different story to fully accept it, on an emotional level.

Some of my journaling spiraled off in new directions, not totally related to a previous healing session. I see that as an experience of the ripple effect – one new insight leads to another. I realized that one area that needed further exploration was the lack of power that I often felt in my life.

Polio did not make me a victim, and I always hated that concept. I saw myself as having great strength in how I dealt with its after-effects. I concentrated on all my strengths – my intelligence, my ability to work with people in solving their problems, my compassion. What I did not recognize was the powerlessness I felt in having contracted the disease in the first place. I viewed it as something that had happened to me. It was being handed a lemon of a life. I had the choice to make lemonade out of it, but I thought I did not have the ability to say "no, thank you" to the lemon, before polio came into my life. In other words, I did not know that I had made the choice to live with this disease.

The concept of our having the ability to make our own choices, of having a free will, came to the surface of my life during these weeks. We do not live in a world of pre-determination, where choices are made and placed upon us. Each of us has the power to make choices, choices profoundly affecting how we live each moment. We have choices in every aspect of our being – physical, emotional and spiritual. In the physical world, I could live my life as a victim, covering up my physical deformities, feeling sorry for myself that I have such a difficult cross to bear. Or, I could choose to live a full and meaningful life, recognizing all the possibilities available to me. In my emotional world, I could choose to view my body in a loving way, or in a despicable way. I could feel pity for myself, or love every aspect of who I am. On a spiritual level, I could express gratitude to Spirit for the gift of polio, or I could choose to rant and rave against Spirit, pleading for a better life than the one I was "given."

We also have free will when we learn to recognize and utilize, the Divine Power surrounding us. Or we can choose to ignore that part of our being. Reiki had given me knowledge, and experience, in working with the Universal Life Force healing energies that are accessible to everyone. Using Reiki expanded my awareness of chakras and energy fields, and the choices I make in my daily life fill those fields with light or with darkness.

Charles has been by my side for years, nudging me into finding the strength and power within myself. It takes a very strong belief to acknowledge I have choices to make in healing myself. It is not about being pretty or acceptable to others any more. It is about believing, and knowing, and choosing, to find the power within myself to heal.

I became more specific about what a healing would be for me. I have always wanted to walk normally, and I started to believe that it was a possibility. I started to change the thoughts in my mind. Rather than thinking, "I want to walk normally, without a limp," I changed my thought to, "I walk strongly and with purpose." The idea that the healing could mean more physical improvements was strong, but I also knew that significant healing was already occurring, on the emotional and spiritual levels. I had made the choice to heal, and it was happening.

Lesson #20: We can choose to work with Spirit World in many different ways.

CHAPTER 21

MORE MANIFESTATION!

The physical changes in my legs and feet continued to emerge, slowly and subtly, throughout the spring. One of the most relaxing parts of my day had always been to come home from work, take off my heavy orthopedic shoes, and walk around the house in my socks or slippers – although I had always been instructed to walk very little without my special orthopedic shoes. I started to notice several subtle changes. It seemed my torso was straighter when I walked without my shoes, rather than with them. Since my belief in limitless possibilities was growing, I wondered if, by any chance, my shorter leg had grown in length, becoming closer to the length of my right leg.

During my annual physical examination, I asked my doctor if she could measure my leg lengths. While growing up, a ritual during my doctor's appointments was his pulling a tape measure out of his pocket to measure my legs, from hip joint to ankle bone on each side. Her reply was, "no way, using a tape measure is not accurate," but added she would refer me to an excellent physical therapist who would know how to do accurate measurements.

It had been decades since I'd seen a physical therapist. Old memories flooded me when I saw the exercise tables, and the mats on the floor in the physical therapy unit. The physical therapist asked me the purpose of the referral. He watched me walk with and without shoes; and with and without my cane. He agreed my limp varied little between wearing the orthopedic shoes, and no shoes at all. That statement alone seemed miraculous to me, very different from any I had ever heard, from any medical professional, during the past five decades.

He also laughed about using a tape measure to measure leg

length, stating that practice has been long gone. He explained the kind of x-ray he could order to measure leg length, very different from my childhood experiences of x-rays. Rather than lying on an x-ray table, where leg differences could vary due to how my hips were positioned, I would be standing up, the only true way to see differences in leg lengths.

I told him that my calves and foot muscles had become more defined in the past year, a change that both my husband and I have noticed. His impressions about my limp were that strengthening the muscles in my hips and buttocks would make a major difference – no one had ever told me that before, in all these years. My childhood experiences of physical therapy were focused on my legs and feet. He developed an exercise program for me, using an exercise ball, to strengthen my hip and buttock muscles.

Then he asked me to tell him about my orthopedic shoes. I went into the long, painful story of the special orthopedic shoes that I'd worn since my surgeries in 1960. I explained how my orthopedic surgeon recommended the shoes with a steel shank embedded in the inner portion of leather in each shoe; the addition of arch cookies; the built-up heels, with the left heel being higher than the right, to make my legs the same length while walking.

The physical therapist replied wearing this type of orthopedic shoe was no longer necessary, as my legs and feet were strong enough to wear an orthotic slipped into a "normal" shoe. He explained that orthotics being used for polio victims was a new development in the past five to ten years. In fact, the orthotics would position my feet better, and muscle strength in my feet and legs would probably increase even more.

To describe my reaction as being stunned is an understatement. No one, and I mean, no one – no doctor, or any other kind of medical professional – ever told me that normal shoes would ever be an option for me. It was outside of my realm of possibilities. Even though I thought I was fully immersed in the concept of limitless possibilities, I had not visualized myself in normal shoes, unless, or until, a miracle had occurred and my physical body became "normal" again. I had not expected, at all, that something like this would occur during a physical therapy evaluation. It took my breath away, and the reality did not sink in for a while. We talked more, and I gave him permission to cast my feet for the orthotics during the appointment.

After the session, I came home, flopped down on the bed and sobbed for over an hour, overwhelmed with feelings of disbelief, joy, and gratitude. This was an affirmation of changes occurring in my life, and an affirmation that everything was unfolding just as it was meant to be. I was flooded with childhood and adolescent memories of arguing with my mother every time I needed a new pair of shoes. It was painful for me to wear shoes that looked so different from every other girl's. I had also pleaded with my doctor, for years and years, to please let me wear other shoes, without any success. I hated, hated, HATED those ugly shoes.

As the years went by, and I became an adult, I learned to accept the ugly, old-lady shoes, as I focused on more important things in my life. While the tears occurred less frequently during my adulthood, I had never really shed the belief that having to wear ugly shoes prevented me from looking, and feeling, pretty. I had internalized the ugliness of those heavy orthopedic shoes, as a representation of the perceived ugly parts of me. Being able to buy and wear ordinary shoes, like other women, started to heal this negative image. This was yet another step on my path to full emotional healing.

Another reality that I reviewed was the actual process of buying shoes that I had lived for several decades. As the decades went by, more and more of the orthopedic shoe companies went out of business. For the past fifteen or twenty years, when I needed new shoes, I went to the orthopedic shoe store and chose among a handful - and I mean, handful - of styles, from a catalog. Often, I replaced a worn-out pair of shoes with the same style, as there were no new styles. The shoes were expensive, and adding on the costs of special heels and arches totaled approximately three hundred dollars, all for a pair of shoes I did not like.

Of course, I would need to be selective about the kind of normal shoes that I could wear – no sleek sandals or stiletto heels, but I'd be able to wear sneakers, boat shoes, boots, sturdy sandals, pretty mary janes, and so on. I'd be able to go to a regular shoe store for the first time in my memory. It would be FUN to buy shoes. I cannot remember ever feeling that way before! How exciting and fun my next few weeks became, as I shared my news with my children and other family members, and filled up my closet with normal shoes, and threw away the old orthopedics.

And, of course, I journaled on the fun aspects of this new experience in my life. The paradox that I soon discovered was this: My physical appearance was becoming less important to me, day after day. At the same time, my physical appearance was improving. Obtaining my self-worth through my physical appearance was decreasing. The true essence of me emanated from my spiritual self, and I started to learn that is what really matters in life. I am learning, right now, my biggest life lesson.

Ah, I was living in the happy world of manifesting good things! I started to think of this great news as the "Great Shoe Event." It became a visible, concrete step in my healing process. What surprised me was that I had not specifically manifested being able to wear normal shoes. I was simply manifesting a healing, in whatever way it was meant to be, and received a lovely surprise. I had not considered the possibility of being able to buy normal shoes, unless I received a total physical cure. I started to realize how many different ways healings can occur. There are no limits to those possibilities.

I further honed my desires for healing. I know I am being

called to tell my story and hopefully it will positively affect many people in the world. My musings were all over the place! It seems if I experienced a total physical healing it would grab the attention of many people and teach a profound lesson – everything is possible and there are absolutely no limits, in any realm of healing. I worried that if I only experienced a partial physical healing, it would not garner enough attention in today's overloaded information world to teach important lessons to others. I realized my lifelong dream had been based in a self-centered motive, and the reason for the dream now felt trite and meaningless.

This healing has a greater purpose, and that became my new focus. What exactly must happen to reach and teach other people in today's world? I finally came to the conclusion that only God knows what my healing will encompass, and I simply needed to trust that the purpose would be fulfilled. I needed to quit worrying about the details – God has a better plan in mind, than what I could ever visualize. All I needed to do was to continue my journey and trust that it would all work out perfectly, according to Divine Plan. What parts of my body would be healed was not the important question; the important question was this: "Do I truly believe that anything is possible?"

At the same time, I am still a breathing, living, middle-aged American woman – and if part of the healing has personal benefits for me, so be it! How great would it be to be able to do the physical activities I'd always dreamed of! It would be a wonderful bonus. There is nothing wrong with being pretty and having fun!

It is reconnecting, even more, with that little girl self still living within me, the one who loves to play and be happy. I love to watch little children who experience pure joy when they chase a butterfly or lick an ice cream cone. It is a blessing that all of us sophisticated adults can remember. I am living a blessed life right now, and to have more blessings in my life is a beautiful gift from the Universe. I can have fun and joy, while experiencing the purpose of my life. Life purposes do not always have to be so serious.

By the way, the x-ray showed that my left leg length had not changed. The left leg is still shorter than the right by 3/8", and my normal shoes will still have a small lift on the left shoe. However, in my heart, I know the left leg could still grow, if it is helpful in living out my life purpose. And, I know that other small miracles in my life could occur – miracles that I have not even thought of, but God has planned.

Lesson #21: We receive many blessings when we live our life purpose.

CHAPTER 22

MORE PROCESSING

Some days, it feels like I am living two lives. I am experiencing these tremendously meaningful spiritual events in the intuitive shamanic sessions, followed by rich journeying and writing. How do I tell other people about it? It is so hard to explain to people who may not be open to it. And, what would I say exactly? The physical changes are subtle, and I do not know when, or if, a physical cure will occur. All I am sure of right now is that I am getting stronger, and the physical changes are not over. The emotional healing is monumental, but unless I told a very, very long tale, it is hard to explain (thus, this book). My spiritual awareness is growing in leaps and bounds, but it seems those kinds of discussions can occur with only a few individuals in my life, at specific times. Although there are a few special, accepting people in my life where I am sharing small bits and pieces of my journey, there are dozens more who do not know what I am experiencing.

I am not ready to put it all out there yet for the world to judge. So, it must be fear that stops me – hmmmmm... fear, fear, fear. What am I fearful of? I'm fearful that friends, family members, and acquaintances will not understand, that they will judge that I have gone off the deep end. I'm fearful that because of their religious convictions, they will judge that I've lost my Catholic faith. I'm fearful that I will lose friends. But, if I lose friends over this, were they really friends, after all? I think it will be easier when my healing has reached a miraculous level – even though I know I've already experienced several miracles on this journey. It seems it will be easier to hand them my newly published book – will it? Will they be hurt that I did not have the courage to share my journey with them before I share it with the whole world? It's obvious that my courage needs to be strengthened, before I "go public" with my story.

The Great Shoe Event became the opportunity for me to start sharing my improvements with my children, siblings, aunts and uncles, co-workers and friends. All were happy and excited about my news, and shared their amazement that my legs and feet were improving, after more than half a century of no changes. And, in the early 90s, when I first received the post-polio syndrome diagnosis, I was told the most I could hope for was maintaining what I had. No one foresaw improvement for me. To get better was never considered.

I told them I thought it was the combined yoga, massage and Reiki that really made the difference, and slipped in the fact that I was also seeing a "different kind of healer," purposefully not using the shamanic word. This was not a lie, as I believe the yoga, massage and Reiki played a major role in the physical strengthening. This was not exactly the whole truth either, as I barely mentioned the emotional and spiritual healings that I was experiencing. I'm not quite ready to tell them I am having regular sessions with an intuitive shamanic healer, and that I am doing my own shamanic journeying and healing work between sessions. In the end, I don't think they will really care how it all happened and will share in my joy as the healing continues to occur. I'm getting closer to telling them the entire story, but I am not ready – yet.

I couldn't wait to tell Starr about the Great Shoe Event and scheduled another session with her, a few weeks prior to our daughter's wedding. The momentum was great, and I wanted to make sure I stayed on my healing track. The messages I received that day were simple and clear – it was time to relax, sit back, and simply enjoy. I was told I had been working hard towards my healing, and it was now time to have fun. It was time for my little girl to come out and play. The timing was perfect, as we traveled to California for the joyous day.

A few weeks later, I found fear again. Although Gary's plan was to do massage therapy as his full-time career, both of us found comfort in the steady income of his part-time engineering job. When Gary received a two-week notice from his company that all telecommuting positions would end, my initial reaction was based in fear. My "worry gene" went into overdrive, as I worked out our budget, in my mind, over and over again. In the past, Gary had been laid off several times, and we knew what it felt like to have no steady income when I was a stay-at-home mother, or live on my smaller social worker income. All of these doubts and misguided beliefs generated negative energies.

We discussed how we could deal with this job loss differently this time. Our financial situation was considerably better, as we had known the part-time engineering job could disappear at any time, and we had saved to be ready for this possibility. Within days, we grew in our "trust in the process." Both of us believed if he is meant to be a massage therapist, it would all work out. Of course, that thought is sometimes easier said than done. Doubts and worries would surface in my mind, but I would use positive affirmations to shoosh them away. Processing all of this was a real challenge.

The first week of his not being an engineer held its own small miracles. We had been discussing the opportunities that having extra time gave him – the time to network and build his massage business, and the time to meditate and simply "be." He took time to meditate and visualized new clients coming to his business. Another time, he visualized himself as a healer, not as an engineer.

Then the phone started to ring, even before he had any opportunity to network. By the end of the week, he had completed more massages than he had any other week prior to this one. I had also completed several Reiki sessions with very appreciative and generous clients. And a new practitioner joined our group. In other words, in the first week of having no engineering income, his massage and healing arts business brought in more income in one week, than any other week in the past year. What an affirmation God gave us!

It had been difficult for Gary to live in Spirit while he was working in a profession that no longer fit into his life purpose. We had continued to live with our fears of lack, worrying about how to pay the bills if his steady income disappeared. We had not trusted the Universe enough, and we thought he could not leave his engineering job until his massage business was built up more. All these thoughts and beliefs had generated negative energy.

We had it backwards. He needed to leave the engineering job first, to build his massage practice. When the engineering work left his daily life, Gary was able to shake off the negative vibes of a job that no longer fit him, similar to a dog shaking off the water when he jumps out of a swimming pool. Gary was able to more clearly define himself as a massage therapist, and he attracted clients to him. The last client to call for an appointment that week was a woman for whom he had provided a brief chair massage at a health fair six months earlier. It is no coincidence that this was the week she decided to call him for an appointment. The releasing of the negative energy, and replacing it with positive healing energy, was like a magnet that attracted her to schedule a massage therapy session with him. Living in positive energy created new business for him.

And my personal healing rose to a new level during this time. It seemed Gary's having extra time placed new emphasis on his participation in my physical healing. I remembered Starr's comment – actually, Spirit's comment – that Gary was to be a major part of my healing, and we revisited how that may occur. We discussed it, and both of us spent some time in meditation, to seek further guidance.

Both of us grew in the knowledge there would not be one

specific method of healing for him to use with me, but rather he simply had to follow his intuition and inspiration each time he worked with me. There could be many methods used, and these would probably change over time.

One of us came up with the idea of having weekly healing sessions. So we started these sessions. Some sessions were centered on water – he would send Reiki energies to warm water before I stepped into the bath tub, or he would massage my legs in warm water. Sometimes he would give me a massage after a bath. On the massage table, he would do a regular massage, or stretch my leg muscles, or do Reiki before, during, or after a massage – the list goes on. Each session was unique as Gary simply followed his intuition. He also was inspired to massage my legs every morning with a cream containing rosemary oil. The more open he became to doing different things, the more he was guided to try something new.

Within a few months, both of us saw the results of this work. My leg muscles were growing bigger, again. And my legs actually became straighter! I could feel my posture improving when I walked and, when I remembered, I said positive thoughts to myself when I walked. I saw myself with a straighter back and a less pronounced limp. We discussed these changes and delighted in each one. It was like watching a child grow up, feeling the joy of each new development.

I also found the time to work on my own healing. One night, during meditation, I saw how the polio was still attached to my body. I knew it was time to release the polio. I requested guidance from any Spirit Guide. I visualized polio as a loving part of myself, at the lower part of my spine. I talked to it, just as I would talk to an old friend. I told it I love and appreciate it for being with me all these years, but now it was time to move on. I felt its resistance and its sadness for leaving me. I further explained that it served my life purpose for these years, but now my purpose has changed, requiring it to leave me. I felt it leaving and then realized a small part of it was still attached, and I had to coax that piece to go away too. I sent it great gratitude and love, and then sent Reiki healing energy to my lower back to fill that empty space with love. This reminded me of the time when Starr removed the brown sludge from my leg. What I saw was a small, red, round piece of energy located in my spine.

Another day, I realized that I tensed up my shoulders whenever I walked – I had never been aware of that. It could not be healthy to contain that kind of tension in my body. Many of us carry that kind of stress-related tension with us every day. Whenever I remembered, I would relax my shoulders. It slowly dawned onto me that I had always held my shoulders that way, and it began with using crutches during my childhood years. It became a body part that was called upon to compensate for the weakness in my legs, without actual awareness from me. Even when I no longer used crutches, my shoulders continued to think they needed to carry me.

During one of our evening healing sessions, I asked Gary to help me release that particular tension in my shoulders, and both of us set that intention. As soon as he started massaging my shoulders, my eyes flooded with tears, and the flooding continued while he worked. I was not sad or happy; the release of tears coincided with the release of the tension. Silently, I talked to my shoulders, just as I had talked to my polio a few weeks earlier. I acknowledged them for carrying me for these past decades and expressed my most sincere gratitude. But I told them they can now take a rest and be like other shoulders. My legs were strong enough to carry me now, and they no longer had to compensate for my legs. In my mind's eye, I visualized my body in a more balanced way, the bottom half being as big and strong as the top portion. This was the exact opposite of how I had always pictured myself. My image had always been one of having "football-player shoulders" and skinny, stick-like legs. It was time to release that image.

Both of us were healing our past identities, during these weeks. Gary was healing himself by releasing his old identity of being an engineer, and embracing the new identity of becoming a massage therapist and healer. I was healing myself by releasing old worn-out images, tensions, and energies, working towards seeing myself as a whole person. As a couple, we were healing an aspect of our relationship. This time, when we were facing a new financial challenge, we were releasing old thoughts and beliefs about living in lack. Although our income was less, we learned to embrace abundance. We were embracing a new life of richness, based in living in Spirit, rather than the false promises of money and materialism.

I felt more alive than I had in years. I was slowly shifting my being, from a limited and negative space, to an unlimited-possibility, loving space. Everything was coming together, and I felt healthier than I ever had.

Lesson #22: We live in a world of unlimited possibilities.

CHAPTER 23

ANOTHER EXPERIENCE OF RHYTHM

Rhythm is experienced in many ways in our lives. It was becoming obvious to us that our vacations were more important than simply getting away from our normal workdays to visiting a new place and relaxing. While we still had elements of fun and relaxation, it also seemed more spiritual growth was always experienced. Perhaps leaving the daily hustle and bustle enabled us to become more open to Spirit.

For the past few years, I have become more aware of how the right books find me just when I need them. Some of the books present new knowledge and growth opportunities, while others serve as tools of assimilation for knowledge already learned. As we were preparing for a two-week vacation to Switzerland, several books came to me that proved to be exactly what my healing journey required.

My suitcase contained two books by two different mediums, and it had been at least two years since I read a book written by a medium. I love hearing stories about mediums connecting with deceased loved ones and the healing that is brought to the grief-stricken family members and friends. Every time I read one of these books, it seems I always learn something new. And this time was no different. A comment made by one of the mediums really struck me. She noted each of us can access the healing energies of our ancestors – all we had to do was ask. The ancestors feel honored to be remembered and greatly appreciate our requests for their guidance and help while we are living our lives on earth. I remembered Valerie's statement about how much Dad enjoyed connecting with me through her sessions and how that resonated with me.

One night, while Gary was sleeping next to me, I was thinking about these books and Valerie's comment. I realized how close I feel to my ancestors, and how learning their names and more about their lives, as part of my genealogy work, provided me with a unique opportunity. I decided to call upon my ancestors, by name. I called my parents (Jim and Ginge), and my grand-parents (Adrian and Lucille, and Clarence and Lucy), and my great-grandparents (William and Ella, Louis and Mary, Louis and Emma, and August and Martha). I decided to nickname them "The Fourteen." I also invited any other relatives – especially my baby sister Patty, aunts and uncles, and cousins – to join the session. I invited my Spirit Guides, my angels, or any other spirit or person who loved me. In my mind's eye, I went to Spirit World and visualized myself lying on a quartz table, with my ancestors and loved ones standing around me, beaming me with light and healing energies. My physical body became warm and relaxed. When it seemed the session was ending, I expressed my gratitude for their participation in my healing.

I've repeated similar sessions many times since that initial one. Because these loved ones are no longer encumbered with humanly concerns, their love is totally unconditional, and comes to earth as pure healing energy. The loving connection is stronger than it was on earth, and they understand the many levels of my healing and know where the energy is most needed at any point in time.

Another book in my suitcase was one about quantum physics and healing. A basic quantum physics concept is that thoughts must be attached to emotions if an intention is to manifest. Emotions are the power sources that move us forward in life, and thoughts are the guidance of those power sources. For example, we could decide that a degree in education would ensure a secure living in teaching school children. A college education is not easy, and unless we felt some kind of inspiring emotion to obtain that degree, the intention of obtaining the degree may never happen.

When we combine the thoughts in our minds with the power of emotion, feelings are created. These feelings are either fueled by love or by fear. We could approach teaching through our love for children, or we could approach teaching through fear that it is the only way to find financial security. Our thoughts and feelings create our beliefs.

A written or spoken intention, not based in emotions and beliefs, probably would not manifest. I realized that I had not allowed myself to feel fully what my life would be with a total physical healing. That may sound a little strange since I have spent hours meditating, journaling and writing about my healing. But, I also recognized there were still doubts in my mind and I was scared of fully feeling the emotions associated with a physical cure. I was fearful of setting myself up for a huge disappointment, if the healing did not occur. I was living in the land of "what ifs."

So that night, after Gary fell asleep, I invited "The Fourteen" and my other relatives to help me with that fear. I embarked upon another shamanic journey. I saw myself on the quartz table, and Mom walked up to me and pulled a black stone from my heart. It looked like a piece of shiny black coal. She told me it encompassed all my fears, and she was taking them away from me. As she held the stone in her hands, the other relatives directed healing energies from their hands to the stone, and it transformed into a piece of beautiful white quartz. Mom then placed the white quartz back into my heart. It was a very moving experience and I sent Mom gratitude and love for her gift.

From now on, whenever any doubts enter my mind, I will send the doubts to the Light and remember the loving quartz in my heart.

During our time in beautiful Switzerland, we discovered another healing tool – hot mineral springs. When we arrived in a charming little skiing village, we saw a brochure for a nearby hot mineral springs. Since we had never visited such a place, we decided it would be a unique vacation experience. The water was delicious, the mountains rising around all sides of the pool were unbelievably majestic, and the people were delightful. After being in the warm waters for only a few minutes, I felt sensations in my legs that were new to me. Gary massaged my legs several times underwater, and the sensations lasted for hours. We knew further healing had occurred.

This vacation exemplified the rhythms in life for us. While the original intention for this vacation was to experience another European country and enjoy the break from work and other obligations, our being open to other experiences enriched the trip greatly. I thought there could be times of learning for me, as I chose books to enrich further spiritual knowledge. Along with relaxation and rest came further healing. Along with learning more about spiritual concepts came the experience of living them more fully. While we enjoyed the sightseeing and experiencing the beautiful mountains, lakes and cities of Switzerland, the meaningful experiences of further healing provided our best memories of the trip. On our flight back to the States, we talked about the growth cycles that we experienced, and how it seems our vacations of the past few years had significant occurrences.

Upon our return home, we researched hot mineral springs and their beneficial effects for various diseases and physical conditions. It was striking how many springs there are in the world, and it seems previous generations appreciated their healing effects more than our modern generations do. We also learned how to replicate some of the mineral combinations in our own bathtub. Who knew that Epsom salts had so many benefits? Taking Epsom salt baths became a frequent part of the weekly healing sessions.

So my life continued in the integration of many new and exciting experiences, whether these occurred on a massage table, at a hot springs in Switzerland, or while reading a book at home.

Lesson #23: Life is full of many learning and healing opportunities.

CHAPTER 24

AN EXPERIENCE OF REINCARNATION

It was hard to believe that four months had passed since my last individual healing session with Starr. So many things had happened in my life, a time of relaxation without focus on healing, our trip to Switzerland, and a re-emphasis on healing. I told Starr about continued muscle growth in my calves and feet. When I pulled up my pant legs to show her, she exclaimed, "Your legs are straighter." She was the first person, besides Gary and me, who noticed that change. Of course, I had not really pointed it out to anyone else. And, since I continued to wear slacks or long skirts all the time, it was hard for others to notice.

There were a few minutes of silence while Starr connected with Spirit. When she spoke, she stated she had been informed the task for this session was to visit a past life of mine. She asked for my permission to do so, and I readily agreed. After another time of silence, she explained she had found herself on top of a submarine in a docking area, and it seemed that the men were speaking something like a Norwegian language. She stated she had been guided for me to join her in this scene, where I would be an active participant. She asked me to close my eyes and silently state the intention of joining the scene, while she returned to Spirit World.

The next time she returned, she explained that she had seen the commander of the submarine, and the commander was actually me, in a previous life. He had a limp and used a cane. He was a seafaring fellow, with a beard, and had a gentle persona. The two of us had approached him, and initially he turned and walked away from us, as he thought we were ghosts. Starr explained that we were good people, like angels, and would not harm him. We just wanted to talk to him. She asked me to visualize the entire scenario and imagine myself talking with him.

So I intentionally joined this scene, and I saw it in my mind. The commander and I sat down on a bench, and I reassured him that I only had good intentions. These words were spoken silently in my mind, not out loud. I felt like my counselor-self, and reached out to him and touched his arm. At that moment, Starr said, out loud, "Deb, he really needs a hug, just go ahead and hug him." When I imagined the hug, I felt pure, unconditional love for this gentle man, and I hugged him for quite a while. I asked him about his limp, and he told me the story. Many years ago, he was in a fight with another man, and the other man suffered greater injuries than him. It seemed he felt guilty about hurting the other man so badly. And, he told me the fight was over a woman. I gave him empathy, support and love, telling him that he needs to forgive himself for hurting the other man.

After several minutes of my silent conversation with the gentleman, I came back to the physical world and opened my eyes. Starr's eyes were already opened, and she asked me if we could discuss what each of us learned. She began by stating that the Commander's limp was a result of a fight he was in, approximately thirty years earlier. She intuited the commander was now in his 50s, and the fight had occurred in his 20s. She stated he was in love with a young woman, and he had fought for her honor. But the woman had not been happy about this fight and did not return his love. He was deeply wounded by her rejection and spent the following decades at sea, running away from this pain. Starr stated that the injury causing the limp was to his left hip. She also commented that he is highly regarded by the men on the submarine. Then I told her what my experience had been.

I was stunned by the similarities of the information each of us had learned separately. Starr had more detail than I did, which I attribute to her shamanic healing training and practice. Starr then asked me to return to Spirit World and ask him what he would like his life to be now. As he was telling me his wishes, I visualized his future. He wanted to return to the land, get married, and have a family. I visualized him on a porch, looking like a country gentleman, with a pipe, light cotton shirt, pants and suspenders, and high leather boots. His wife came out onto the porch and greeted him warmly. I knew she had been a widowed lady, who owned this property, and she had grown children. They were very happy, living comfortably, in this land of rolling green hills.

I related this scene to Starr. She suggested that both of us, in Spirit, return to him and show him that this option existed for him. All he had to do was believe that his life could be happy, and he could attain his true desires. He expressed gratitude to both of us – and then walked off, with no limp. He had decided to return to the land, and he had changed his future.

Starr and I left the Spirit World again and discussed what had happened. She explained that because the Spirit World does not know time, as we know it, this gentleman (me) changed the course of that previous life, healing himself. This action would release some of the issues of my current lifetime, enabling me to find further healing now.

Some of the connections from the Commander's life to my current life were unmistakable. The most obvious one, of course, is the limp. His limp could not be released until he released the pain and rejection he had felt because of the woman's disappointment in him. My Spirit gave him the love and support that he had not felt for decades. And the reference to the injury of the left hip also has a correlation in my physical body. The left hip is where I have the lowest levels of calcium in my body.

Starr and I discussed how his living on a submarine for decades was symbolic of the limited-type of thinking that had kept me in bondage for decades. What could be more limiting and suffocating than living in the metal box of a submarine for all those years – or living with my limiting thoughts for all those years? Starr also made a connection between the metal of a submarine and the metal braces that I wore in my early childhood. She also commented that the respect others had for him sounds similar to how people view me now. I also connected to the feelings of rejection that he felt from the woman he loved. I also have experienced rejection in this lifetime, due to my physical appearance and limp.

I was reminded of my strong feelings for the ocean and how relaxed I feel whenever I am on an ocean beach. His living at sea, within a protected capsule, provided him a certain level of peace, although true happiness eluded him during those years. I also related to his feelings of running away. When I experience the pain of rejection, my natural inclination is to simply leave the situation and not have to deal with it, even when that is not a viable option. Over the years, I learned to fight that inclination as I know it is not a healthy emotional response.

I spent the next days and weeks reflecting on this previous lifetime of mine, and worked on healing all the feelings, thoughts and beliefs that followed me into this lifetime.

While my belief in reincarnation had been growing the past few years, this session made the belief of reincarnation become even more real for me. I had felt strongly connected to the Commander, and I believe his life had been a previous life of mine. I had actually felt his emotions, as if they were my own – it was more than a compassionate response from my heart. It was quite an interesting conversation that we had – I felt his emotions and my emotions at the same time!

Reincarnation is simply the belief that all of us are spirits who choose to come to planet earth multiple times to incarnate in physical bodies. The purpose is to learn necessary lessons through various life experiences. These lessons are not easy and may take many lifetimes to fully grasp. All of us must be the betrayer and the betrayed, the master and the servant, the teacher and the student. We have karmic debts to repay and karmic blessings to receive. As our souls experience more lifetimes, we evolve into human beings where giving unconditional love and selfless service to others become our life plans.

Towards the end of this session, I told Starr I had been struggling, yet again, with thoughts about a physical cure vs. healing on emotional and spiritual levels. Starr checked with Spirit and was told our next session should be held outdoors to heal even deeper emotional issues. She suggested that I may be holding onto anger as a result of having polio. My initial reaction was that this statement did not resonate with me. While I have had moments of anger associated with the limitations I experienced from the polio, feelings of sadness and fear resonate stronger. However, I told Starr I would keep an open mind, and journal several times before our next session, working to discover the deeper emotions that still lie within me.

Lesson #24: We are spiritual beings, living in physical bodies.

CHAPTER 25

MORE ON REINCARNATION

Our jaunt to a secluded setting could not have happened on a prettier autumn day in the mountains of western North Carolina. I was excited to follow the directions of Spirit and have a session in the woods. Since our move to Asheville, I have become increasingly aware of the healing energies of the earth. I have also read a number of books and articles about the Cherokee tribe, one of the Native American tribes in this area. Their beliefs and stories reflect a personal connection and appreciation of the earth and its spirits, a connection that is being rediscovered and appreciated by the rest of us.

Starr began our session by finding the "right" spot among the trees and creating sacred space through burning sage, smudging the earth and both of us. Then we closed our eyes, and I felt peace and calmness. When we talked a few minutes later, Starr reported she had immediately seen a circle of many Native American Spirits surrounding us.

I shared with Starr the findings of my journaling over the past several weeks. What I had discovered was the pure terror I felt when the polio struck me, at the age of 3 years and 2 months. I was too young to verbalize how very scared I felt as I did not have the language to express these emotions. I had always been told I woke up one morning and could no longer stand up. Through my journaling, many emotions were brought to the surface. I remembered the events, on an emotional level, for the first time. I wrote about how one day, I had been running all over the house and outdoors, like a typical three-year-old. The next day, I could not stand up and I was scared to death. I thought maybe I was dying. Then I realized how upset and sad all the adults around me were and that scared me even more!

During the journaling in the past few weeks, I frequently became overwhelmed by the intensity of these feelings. I had to stop writing several times, just to catch my breath and calm myself. I knew these feelings had been suppressed when I was very young, as I did not have the language to express them. And more importantly, the feelings were just too big and scary to revisit during my childhood. I had suppressed these feelings to the point that I was not even aware of them.

Starr went to Spirit World and received directions for the session. She had been directed to take me to the Temple of Akashic Records, and she asked me if I had ever visited this place. I told her about the time I visited the Temple, during the psychic development classes in Pittsburgh. I explained how we were taught to visualize the Temple, with its tall white pillars gracing the portico, and the steps leading up to the front door. During that exercise, I was guided to walk to the correct row and book, my Akashic Record. She liked this image and directed me to visualize the Temple again, ask to be guided to my book, and to the lifetime that would be most helpful to me now.

I visualized walking up the steps of the large, white Temple, opening the door, and actually seeing my Akashic Records Guide. He greeted me warmly, as if we were old friends, and walked me down the large main aisle. I was surprised when he took me to an aisle on the right, about a third of the way down (I remembered going to the left side before, towards the back) but decided to let that thought go. We stopped in front of a large book, and I opened it.

What I saw was startling! It reminded me of a children's pop-up book, but this scene was alive. There was a huge fire, and flames and smoke leapt out. Immediately, I felt very scared and upset, and I told Starr what I was seeing. She asked me questions, and I told her the following story, as I was receiving the information. (This was a different process, than earlier sessions with Starr, when I went back and forth between Spirit World and the physical world. This time, I related the scene as I experienced it. I think it would have been too scary for me to be in the Spirit scene alone.)

I was a Native American woman who had gone off into the woods, gathering food for my family, and was walking back towards my village. Then I saw huge flames and smoke in the distance. I dropped my basket and ran as fast as I could towards the village. I saw other villagers running away from the smoke. Soon I was unable to move any closer to the village, due to the heavy smoke and intense heat. I had to back away and run in the opposite direction. Somehow, I became separated from the other people of the village. I was very upset and terrified that I would not see my family again. I did not know if they had made it out alive.

I was walking along a path in the woods, looking down, feeling very upset, trying to decide what to do next. I had no home and was not sure if my family was still alive. A mountain lion sprang from the forest and attacked me. I had just a moment of terror, and then complete and utter serenity – I immediately knew the lion had killed me. I floated out from my body and over the village, only to see piles of smoldering ashes. Although I felt lost, I continued to float around and around. A sense of calmness engulfed me as I floated above the village, but I also remained frantically worried about my family. I did not know if they were dead or alive.

When I related this scene to Starr, she asked my spirit to go and find my family. I found them immediately, in a temporary village with other survivors of the fire. I saw my young husband and two young children, and I realized the husband from that lifetime was Gary, my husband in this lifetime. He was very sad, as I had not returned from my foray into the woods, and he assumed I was dead. He was very worried about how he would be able to raise the children on his own.

Starr instructed me to talk to him, to let him know I was present with him in spirit. I appeared to him, talked to him about his ability to be a good father, and reassured him all would be well. I told him I would be next to him and guiding him over the years. I also held my children, and I did not want to leave the scene. I felt great love for the three of them. When I told Starr about my reluctance to leave, she reassured me that all would be well, and it was time to leave this lifetime, close the book, and return to the Temple.

I floated away from my family and returned to the Temple. I closed the large Akashic Record and simply laid down on the floor, too exhausted to move. The Guide, and other Spirits, knelt beside me and sent me healing energies through their hands. After a few minutes, I stood up, expressed my gratitude to them, and walked out of the Temple.

Starr and I discussed the importance of this event, and we agreed it had great relevance to my feelings of terror. I thought of the day when polio struck me, and the feelings were significantly less intense than the strong feelings I had experienced during my recent times of journaling. But, I also knew that the terror was not totally healed, and I would need to do more work with this emotion. She reminded me I could visit the Akashic Records as often as needed, on my own, to further heal the terror that existed within me.

It was very significant to me that my last two sessions with Starr had been experiences of visiting previous lifetimes. I realized how certain aspects of previous lifetimes had been reenacted in my current life. Or, to put it another way, I was obtaining more information as to why I chose to have experiences in this lifetime to heal difficult past emotions. It was a reinforcement of my belief that I had chosen to have polio, a belief I had as a child, long before accepting the concept of reincarnation. I needed to heal these emotions, once and for all. I was thrilled to learn that Gary and I had shared at least one previous lifetime – and actually, it has probably been several lifetimes, as we've always felt a deep connection to each other.

The next several weeks, I took shamanic journeys on my own and visited the Records several times. The first three times, I relived various horrific scenes, in different places and lifetimes. I was always able to revisit the scenes and resolve those experiences with peaceful endings. Even when I died, I revisited in spirit and reassured others that I was in a peaceful place. Just as I did with my Native American husband, I brought messages of peace to my grieving loved ones who still remained on earth.

Then the fourth time I visited the Records, I visited a memory that was different. In that scene, I was a male Native American warrior. I stood at the edge of a large field, with my legs planted strongly on the earth, and my arms folded across my chest. I was watching a fire, with large billows of gray smoke. I knew I had started the fire, for a worthy purpose, and the fire was controlled and necessary for next year's plentiful crops. I felt satisfied and pleased that the fire was burning exactly as planned. At that moment, I knew that the deep terror I had been carrying around for the past fifty years (not to mention, numerous lifetimes) was healing. I expressed gratitude to the Akashic Records Guide, my Spirit Guides, my loving ancestors and relatives, and any other Spirit who joined me on this part of my journey.

Little by little, I was becoming my own healer. I was becoming more and more comfortable in doing my own shamanic journeys. It became easier, with Divine guidance, to interpret and find the meanings of the journeys. I also realized that my work was similar to past life regression therapy, an area of work that is now gaining recognition. Gaining knowledge of past lives can be helpful to heal the emotional wounds that we've brought into this life, or heal new wounds created by our need to heal certain emotional parts of ourselves.

So belief in reincarnation is more than simply accepting the fact that all of us have lived before. It can be intentionally experienced for a worthwhile purpose: to bring resolution, healing and peace to our current lives, and our souls, eventually bringing more peace to the lives of our loved ones. When we ask for spiritual guidance and protection, Spirit will reveal aspects of previous lives at the right time, in the right way. We can choose to utilize this belief to propel ourselves into further spiritual understanding and growth. Or, we can choose to live in fear and not take advantage of this helpful information. One caution: if we decide to pursue this path, we should always begin under the guidance of someone experienced and comfortable in this work. And I know, from experience, if the right intention is set, the right person will come into your life, at exactly the right time!

Lesson #25: God places the right people in our lives at the right time.

CHAPTER 26

REFLECTION

Throughout these months, Gary continued his weekly healing sessions with me. And every week was different. He would meditate sometime during the day or early evening, prior to our session, and use his intuition to guide what method he'd use during the session. He was guided to utilize a variety of combinations of massage in hot Epsom salt water, regular massage and Reiki. He could see that some muscles were already larger and stronger than he had ever seen. He also could see that some other muscles were hardly being used. Because they had been weak for so many years, I had learned to "favor" them, barely using them at all, which only contributed to their continued atrophied state. In some cases, they were used in awkward positions, adding to my limp. As I tried using muscles in more normal ways, my awareness of my physical body continued. My days, in most ways, continued a normal lifestyle. Very few people knew all the experiences that were occurring in my spiritual life. As I intended to live a balanced life, I conscientiously focused on ways to balance the physical, emotional and spiritual sides of my being. At times, it seemed my physical healing was not keeping up with my emotional growth, or vice versa. I often had to remind myself that everything was occurring exactly as it was supposed to – all I had to do was remain open to new possibilities and cooperate with messages when I received them from God. I reminded myself if any other healers were part of my process, they would be introduced to me at the right time.

One day at work, one of our physicians introduced me to a chiropractor who was visiting our agency. This chiropractor utilized some alternative methods and energy work. This non-traditional chiropractor, Sarah, and I felt an immediate connection, and I knew I needed to learn more about her alternative techniques. A few weeks later, Gary and I met with her to learn about her work. Because many of her techniques focused on nerve and muscle stimulation, it seemed these could be helpful to me.

Soon I had my initial assessment appointment with Sarah. The session began with my standing on a small platform, leaning into the chiropractic table. As I held onto each side, the table slowly moved forward into the horizontal position, and the platform fell away. Sarah sees how the body holds itself, and detects problem areas, such as differences in leg lengths. She immediately saw that the left leg was shorter than the right leg, as well as other places that were not aligned properly.

Sarah explained that she uses an Activator, a handheld device that gently realigns the spine and joints with a very low force thrust. Energy blocks within the body develop from repressed emotions, beliefs and patterns that can be held for months, years, and even lifetimes. Adjustments can help to liberate this stuck energy, allowing the nervous system to dissipate the blocks.

Sarah detected emotional blocks near my spine and pelvic bones. She asked questions about the onset of polio, and how it felt being a child with limited physical capabilities. As I talked about my feelings, she placed the Activator on particular muscles, releasing the tension and tightness within the muscles. I could feel the tight muscles suddenly becoming more relaxed.

She explained it was obvious I had already completed a significant amount of emotional healing, as we were able to deal with old, deep feelings so quickly. Her explanation agreed with my belief system. As each emotional layer is healed, a deeper layer arises, available for its own healing. We discussed how cells, muscles, bones and the entire body have memories, and one of my tasks would be to release these memories. When released, new neural pathways could develop, resulting in new ways of standing and walking.

After the session, I sat in a chair to regain my equilibrium. Sarah asked for permission to use energy healing on my legs. When I agreed, she sat on the floor and placed both hands on one leg, then the other. Great warmth emanated from her hands, like Reiki energy, and she received several messages.

One message was that my legs had picked up a large amount of negative energy from the steel braces that I wore for the first four years after polio struck, prior to the surgeries. But these energies were now being healed. Also she received the message that my legs were changing a great deal, and that changes would continue. I was certainly amazed by the steel reference, reminding me of Starr's comments during the recent session with the commander/me having lived in a submarine during a past life.

My next days were spent in reflection. I slowly became aware of the reality that my inner emotional and spiritual lives become fully manifested in my physical body. As my feelings about my polio experience had become trapped within my muscles and cells, my physical body was unable to heal itself. My body had not experienced physical improvements for many years, as my feelings and beliefs had not changed. But as these feelings and beliefs started to heal, my physical body was also able to heal.

I recognized all the connections between the many layers of my being, and the connections between all the healers that appeared in my life. Yes, I had to agree to participate in their various techniques and insights. Being human, the doubts still arose within me, from time to time, but those doubts became dimmer and dimmer, as one healer after another had similar messages for me. It was becoming more and more obvious to me.

My next appointment with Sarah was one week later. I had made the decision to deal with whatever came up, no matter how painful or scary it might be. An emotion came to the surface immediately – it was strong, unresolved anger. My first thought was, "oh no, could Starr have been right about anger?" Again, I wanted to deny the fact that I had lots of anger within me. I told Sarah anger does not resonate with me, but sadness and frustration did. Through her asking the right questions, we realized that what I had always called frustration was actually a cover-up for strong anger. I promised Sarah I would journal on the possibility of having anger within me over the next days and weeks. I knew if more healing was to occur in my life, the time had come to face whatever emotions still lay within me.

It is what it is. Finally, finally, finally, I discovered the anger that had resided within me for many years. It originated in my earlier childhood years, from the age of 3 years, until the pre-adolescent years. It seemed that once I hit my adolescent years, I gave myself permission to be a typical teenage girl, with an overprotective mother, to give voice to that anger. And, boy, did I! I had argued, and argued, for pretty shoes, not walking with crutches, going out with friends, over so many things. I had felt the anger, and I did not mind expressing it. I was angry that I did not have boyfriends and could not walk or run like a typical teenager. My anger was expressed through these adolescent rages and through many crying fits. What I had never recognized, or dealt with, was the anger from the first days of having polio and the subsequent early years. Those years had been difficult for me, too. It had become easier and acceptable for me to think about these times with sadness.

Through my journaling, I realized that anger had been scary to me, as a little girl. I had many memories of my mother expressing her anger at various things in her life – and, it had scared me to death! She screamed, she yelled, she threw things – it was scary. It was safer, to me, not to feel the anger. But, it was safe to feel sad. So, I suppressed the anger and became sad instead. Small amounts of anger were expressed through frustration, at specific incidents.

Healing this primal anger became a new intention for me, as

I realized this emotion had to be healed, too. I had to revisit this anger, feel this anger and heal this anger. It was raw and it was painful. It rose to the surface and Gary and I used Reiki energies to heal it. The releasing felt wonderful and we intentionally replaced the spaces of anger with new feelings of love and peace.

I also realized, through journaling, that I had developed beliefs for myself about anger and had become judgmental about this emotion. Although I believed in the adage "feelings are not right or wrong, they just are," I had not accepted this belief for myself. I had seen anger in a negative light, not recognizing that anger is appropriate to certain situations. I had not accepted the fact that I needed to express my anger.

I had made the decision many years ago that I did not want to be one of those people who emanated anger – the kind of person who walks into a room and everyone knows she is angry. Over the years, I had met many angry people, and worked with many in therapy sessions. I was especially sensitive to people who were angry about a disease or physical condition. While I provided empathy and therapeutic skills to facilitate better coping skills, I had made a conscientious decision not to become "one of those angry people." It was a deliberate choice not to live my life in anger, and I pursued emotional acceptance of my chronic condition. In other words, I had made judgments about anger and had been resistant to accepting that I was still holding onto anger myself.

During a later session with Sarah, another emotion, a fear, arose to be healed. The previous day, Asheville had had a few inches of snow. As Sarah was working on my back, we discussed the snow, and she felt a strong emotion rise to the surface. Through her asking the right questions, I recalled many instances of falling on snow and ice throughout my life. I told her about falling in the schoolyard and in parking lots. I related my worst memory – the time I slipped on an icy sidewalk while carrying our baby daughter. Although our daughter had not been hurt, as she landed in a pile of snow next to the sidewalk, the tears flowed as I remembered that terrible day when I had cried inconsolably for hours and hours. After the tears, I again found the blessings in the fact that she had not been hurt.

Sarah took a few moments and reported that she saw several angels standing on either side of me, holding me up by my arms. They told her to reassure me they have always supported me and will continue to support me, and there is no reason to fear falling again. I actually felt the fear rising out of my body. It felt like a load of bricks floating away.

I continued to have sessions with Sarah, and the emotional releasing continued. Releasing emotional blocks in my lower back area enabled my back to stretch further, enabling my walk to become a little straighter. I continued to journal, and to have healing sessions with Gary.

I was continuing on my path of healing, taking it step by step, day by day. I spent hours reflecting on how connected my mind, body and spirit really are. Mind, body, spirit connection became a reality, not just a philosophy. All the changes that were happening in my life reflected and affected each other. I knew it was all good.

Lesson #26: True healing occurs in mind, body and spirit.

CHAPTER 27

DIVINE FLOW

It had been awhile since I had a shamanic healing session with Starr, and it seemed the time was right for another session. Starr immediately saw my recent physical improvements as I walked across the room. She wondered out loud why I felt a need for a session, as my healing was progressing so well. I explained that although I journey frequently on my own now, and most of the time it felt like I was doing exactly what I was supposed to be doing, I felt uncertain at other times. It was not easy for me to totally trust my own intuition and the messages I received or "thought" I was receiving. When I said that it seemed right to simply "check in" with Spirit World, with her assistance, she agreed that it is a good thing to work with other people periodically, to maintain balance.

I shared with Starr that while Gary and I had continued to have regular healing sessions, I had some intuitive feelings that she and Gary were supposed to work with me together, but I could not perceive any other details. However I believed I would receive further guidance when the time was right.

Starr began with a short prayer, closed her eyes, and began the journey into Spirit World. A few minutes later, she reported the session began with Pure Divinity – Jesus Himself. He told Starr that the time is almost here for more healing for me, and it would occur before Easter. While He affirmed I had been doing everything I had been guided to do in the past, it was now time to do some new things, and He gave us some new directives.

The first was for me to find, or buy, a blue crystal as it will also play a part in my healing process. He said it would remind me of water, and that water would also be a part of more healing. I would know the right crystal when I saw it.

Starr saw Jesus walking over to me and washing my feet in water. He showed Starr another scene where He was burying my feet in dirt. He told her this would be happening to me, by a person on earth, but in spiritual reality, it would be Him doing this ritual.

When Starr gave me this information, I was stunned – yet again. I told her that Gary and I were planning a trip in a few months to New Mexico and California. We had been reading the tourist information, and there were two places already on our itinerary. The first place was a sacred site, named El Santuario de Nuestro Senor de Esquipulas, in Chimayo, New Mexico. Chimayo is a small village, located between Santa Fe and Taos. Although I sometimes doubt the legitimacy of such places, this one had rung true with me, and I could not wait to visit it.

The legend of this site is quite interesting. In 1810, a local farmer saw a light emanating from the soil in his field. He dug into the soil, until he found the source of the light, a crucifix. It seemed right to take the crucifix to a nearby church, but then he would find it again, in his field. After this happened twice, he and the other villagers decided to build a chapel around the site where the crucifix was originally found. Soon people traveled to this chapel and found that covering themselves with the dirt led to miraculous healings. Today there is still a sacred pit where visitors can cover their feet with the soil. Many crutches and braces hang on the walls of the chapel. My hope was that I would have the opportunity to have my feet covered with the dirt from this shrine. Shivers ran up my spine when Jesus referred to burying my feet in dirt. The second place we planned to visit was a hot mineral springs, near this chapel.

When Starr returned to Spirit World, Jesus had yet more instructions for the next two months. He instructed Starr that she and Gary were to have a healing session with me in mineral water. She knew the three of us needed to plan an outing to Hot

Springs, NC, about an hour's distance from Asheville, before our trip to New Mexico. (An aside – Gary and I visited Hot Springs for the first time the previous month, for our 35th wedding anniversary. Just like the hot springs in Switzerland, the waters felt great on my legs and feet that day, especially when Gary was massaging them.)

The third time that Starr returned to Spirit World, Jesus had yet more instructions for us. She was to have a sacred ceremony with me. He said that I would have a "major shift" over the Easter weekend, and this ceremony should occur just prior to, or during, the holiday weekend. He showed Starr an anointing with oil, which would signify a "going forth" type of ceremony. Both of us were reminded of various Biblical scenes and Christian traditions when oil has significant meaning. In the Catholic Church, oils are used in the sacraments of Baptism and Confirmation, and these are called chrism oils. Jesus told Starr that I was to select an oil for this ceremony, and it did not need to be an official chrism oil. I knew I'd receive guidance, at the right time, to buy the correct oil.

He also told Starr to be "prepared for a miracle." That message was directed to Starr specifically. Both of us saw that comment as an affirmation to her for her work – and that my healing was only the beginning of more powerful healings in her future work with other people. His Divine Spirit walked over to me, where He embraced me and emanated pure, unconditional love. Then, He walked over to Starr and gave her that special embrace too.

So now we knew why I had felt directed to have another session with Starr. The healing was progressing rapidly now. Everything was connected – my physical changes, my emotional releases, and my spiritual journey. I was thrilled there were connections between my religious upbringing, and my non-traditional spiritual journey. The two were coming together in a most powerful, miraculous way. I always knew, deep within my bones, that the Catholic Church held the Truth – but unfortunately the fears of men have tried to regulate and legislate its powers. True healings still occur – and I can receive messages directly from the Source, just like every other person on earth. Isn't that the original meaning of faith? How did personal faith and religious practice become so convoluted and confusing?

My heart filled with gratitude for this rich experience. I knew Jesus would be with me (as He always was) over the next weeks in a very special way. While I was excited for the changes in my body and spirit, I became even more excited about the "going forth" ceremony.

When the disciples received the blessings and power of the Holy Spirit on Pentecost Sunday, it was not simply to make them holy. It was to give them the power to spread the Word of God to other people. In the same way, the purpose of my healing is to bring the message of healing to others. It was never about me, and I became more and more detached from the desire for a physical cure. I became focused on the purpose of my journey – it is simply to bring the message of Divine Healing to other people. I do not foresee all the details, but I know the telling of my story is important. In fact, I am humble enough to say it will be powerful – not because of me, but because Spirit has designed it to be powerful in whatever ways Spirit has designed to make it powerful. I don't know if it will be significant for a few people, or many people, but it will help others in some way.

I really started to feel a shift within myself, more strongly than ever before, that my life purpose has always been this - to live through the polio experience, and heal myself, with Divine Assistance, over the next fifty years. My life purpose is to demonstrate to others that healing is unlimited and available to all persons. With the help of God, all of us have the power to heal – ourselves, others, and the earth. It was becoming crystal clear to me.

I developed a plan for the following six weeks. I decided to have a few more sessions with Sarah, so that my physical body will be as ready as it can be for the changes to come. I will journey frequently so that Jesus and other Spirits will continue to guide me along my path. I will buy the crystal and the oil. I will dream of my healing, and I will dream about how my healing will positively affect other people. I will feel the emotions and visualize the dream. I will meditate on the many wonderful experiences I have already had. I will meditate on the phrase that was given to me many months previously – "Believe and it is true." This is simply living in Divine Flow.

At the same time, I will work at my job, cook our meals, and connect with our family and friends. I will live my normal life, but I will also live in alignment with Spirit World. We will continue to finalize plans for our New Mexico/California vacation. My heart is filled with gratitude, love and joy. Living in Divine Flow is living fully in the physical world, and living fully in the spiritual world.

Sometimes, it is hard to believe this is really happening. I've always believed in the miracle of healing, but how many people knew a miracle was in the works for them? How many people played an active role in making the miracle happen? What a blessing!

Lesson #27: Living in Divine Flow is living fully in the physical world and living fully with Spirit.

CHAPTER 28

MANY BLESSINGS

When we live within Divine Flow, blessings always occur. We are aware of our spiritual path, and we can choose to cooperate with it fully. Although we may have moments of doubt, we give our intuitive messages and spiritual guidance full credence. We ride along with the flow, and we are blessed in unexpected ways.

About a week before our planned outing to Hot Springs, Starr and I had a brief session, just to check in with Spirit. Starr shared with me she had already received a specific directive for herself several days earlier. She had been directed to begin a major body cleansing which involved fasting from all foods, and drinking a special cleansing liquid, for ten days. She was already in the fourth day of that practice.

I had made some preparations too. I had found my blue crystals, a sparkling blue crystal rock and a blue crystal necklace. I had found my anointing oil too, in a very special way. One of my coworkers sells essential oils, and I borrowed her huge reference book listing dozens and dozens of essential oils, describing their properties and uses. Asking for guidance before I opened the book, I carefully scanned the book and came across an essential oil named angelica. Angelica is sometimes referred to as "oil of the Holy Spirit," and I knew this was the one I was supposed to buy. It would enhance my new purpose – to bring the message of healing to others. For some reason, my coworker's company no longer carried this oil, so I told her angelica was the oil I needed to buy, and I would purchase it elsewhere.

A few days later, this coworker came to my office with a bottle of angelica oil. She said she felt called to go to a local store and buy it for me. She would not accept payment. To me, this was yet another affirmation that many people have been, and continue to be, involved in my healing. I saw her thoughtfulness to buy the oil and present it as a gift as another blessing on my path.

I also journeyed a number of times since the last session with Starr, four weeks earlier. Most often, the person who came to me in the journey was Jesus. He always emanated unconditional love and peace. I wavered between not putting any expectations on the evening, and feeling certain something miraculous would occur. The miracle could be a spiritual healing only – and that would be great. It seemed more physical healing may come too. I felt excited and was learning my biggest lesson of trust yet.

Being a planner, I had wondered about the details and had questions regarding our trip to Hot Springs. I did not know if I should do any kind of meditation or spiritual practice the days before the trip. I also had wondered if I should eat healthier than I usually do, or make any other preparations. I did not know how to bring up the payment issue – how much should we pay Starr, when should we give her money, etc. But I thought I was getting too worried about the details and needed to let things unfold. I did not relate any of these thoughts to Starr before she started the session.

Starr and I went to the Spirit World. I intentionally chose not to journey, allowing Starr to obtain the specific information. What I experienced was a feeling of being surrounded by pure peace and love.

Starr reported that Jesus came to her immediately, and He gave more directions for the following Wednesday evening. He began by saying healing is as simple as believing it is possible and showed her the miracle of the woman touching His cloak and being healed. The purpose of the directions He gave was to affirm and touch our human way of understanding. Jesus asked that we maintain noble silence honor during the drive, meaning we should only talk when necessary and not engage in unimportant conversation. He also told Starr that we were to get the money part taken care of, before the drive, so it was out of the way. Since we were picking up Starr at her apartment, she stated it would be good for me to pay her there, and she would leave the money on her altar at home. That felt so right to both of us.

Jesus also directed me to be very mindful of everything I eat for at least three to four days before Wednesday. He told Starr that she was fasting for both of us, as I needed to have a high energy level for what would occur. It would be no problem to eat extra-healthy and drink lots of water, and forgo sweets for a few days.

When Starr came back to the physical world and verbalized these directions, I told her Jesus had just answered all my questions! Everything He brought up I had already thought about – what an affirmation of the strong connections I am developing with Spirit World. I then related the story of the angelica oil. Starr reported that Jesus simply smiled, as I told her the story.

Starr checked in one more time, and she received directions that surprised both of us. Two days later, Starr was planning another shamanic journeying workshop in our center's space. Jesus told her I needed to participate in a different way this time. I was not to go on my own individual journey, but rather it would be an opportunity for me to "practice" with a group. Starr's routine was to hold Sacred Space for the participants, check in on their journeys and make notes of what she saw. I was to do the same thing. He said that soon I would be called to do a similar, but different, type of healing work with people.

Two days later, Starr held the group journeying workshop. I did as instructed and sat up, while the participants were lying on the floor, with eyes closed. My eyes were closed most of the time, so that I could visit each person's journey. After each visit, I opened my eyes and wrote notes. As usual, each person shared their experience and Starr shared her notes – and the two experiences always correlated well. My excitement grew, as I realized that my notes also correlated. Like Starr, sometimes I saw the same visual experience, and other times, I saw a scene that had a similar message for the participant. After the sharing, Starr explained to the group that I was "practicing" for the first time and asked if I wanted to share my notes. So I did. The affirmations that the participants gave me were yet another sign that I am on the path I am meant to be.

In the late afternoon of the appointed day, Starr, Gary and I headed up to Hot Springs for our healing ceremony. During the entire day at work, I lived in anticipatory excitement. Whenever I began to feel anxious, I repeated the mantra given to me by the Spirit in one of the earlier shamanic healing sessions. "Believe and it is true, believe and it is true, believe and it is true." The anxiety would disappear for a while. I was not anxious due to fear, but rather I simply did not know what to expect.

We picked Starr up at her home and took care of the payment, just as directed. Our drive was quiet and peaceful, although it was a windy, cloudy and cool afternoon in the mountains. Stepping into the hot mineral water felt wonderful to the three of us.

Starr stated that Jesus had given her many messages and directives during the past few days, and His Presence was with us. After a brief prayer where she requested my physical healing, asking for the ability to walk in beauty and grace, she was directed to use the angelica oil. She placed the oil on her fingertip and touched it to the foreheads of each of us.

She was directed to have me lay on my back. She and Gary placed their hands under the water, on my back, for several minutes. We then changed positions, where I laid my head on Gary's chest, while both of his hands held my hips, to keep them underneath the surface of the water. Starr placed her hands on several areas of my back, legs and feet. I could feel the healing energies coming from their hands. Several times, my body visibly shook with all the strong energies pouring into it. An extraordinary sense of calmness and peacefulness filled me, and surrounded me.

At one point, we took a brief break. Jesus told Starr to instruct me to focus on the shifts that were occurring in my DNA and in the memories of my cells for the remainder of the session. He said that everything is shifting for me. I was happy to have something specific to focus on. When Gary and Starr removed their hands for the last time, she had more information for both of us.

She had heard the phrase, "She is healed, she is healed, she is healed" repeated over and over, during the last time she held my feet. My next task would be to reprogram my body to walk in a normal way, to respond to the healing that had occurred. She said it would be like a kind of physical therapy, but it did not need to be a formalized exercise program. I needed to practice and practice. She gave both of us the directive that Gary needed to stop doing so many physical things for me, so that I could build up my strength more. Also, I needed to depend on him less for physical support, teaching my legs and feet that they are strong enough to carry me. This is the exact opposite of the pattern we had established, which was only exacerbated by the post-polio changes that had occurred in the early 90s. It would take a conscientious effort, on both our parts, to change the patterns we had developed over the thirty-five years of our marriage.

So, no, my legs did not change their shape or looks immediately, yet all of us knew that something momentous had happened. I truly believed the healing was complete, and the emotional and spiritual aspects of my being had been healed. My physical body simply had to catch up! Even my physical healing was going to be a process, not unlike my emotional and spiritual healings. It had taken decades for me to reach this point, and I would not experience the full aspects of healing for some time to come. I knew physical improvements would continue, and it was not important what level of "normalcy" I would reach.

All of us expressed deep gratitude for His blessings upon us. We stayed in the water for several minutes, to become grounded in the real world. All three of us felt a little spacey, as we had connected so strongly to the Divine. It was one of the most profound and deep spiritual experiences of my life.

On the drive back, we discussed the timing of this event, as we were towards the end of the Lenten season, quickly approaching Easter. I shared my childhood experiences of Lent. In our household, Lent was a six-week period that was different than any other time of the year. Our nightly sweet treats were gone, as we children "gave up" candy, ice cream, cake and other goodies. On Friday nights, we attended the Stations of the Cross in our small Church. We counted down the days to Easter Sunday when our baskets overflowed with chocolate and other candies. In some ways, the limitations of my physical body had felt like a Lenten experience. I had been denied the ability to walk normally and participate in many sports and physical activities, and now the blessing of an "Easter Sunday" in my physical life was becoming a reality.

Starr's having been directed to fast for ten days also had some similarities to my previous experience with Lent. She shared that because the fasting was a preparation for this event, she had felt honored to participate in this way. At the same time, she had also grown in her own spirituality and knew there were lessons she had learned. It was a healing experience for her too.

We also discussed the timing of our upcoming vacation to New Mexico in a few days. Like Asheville, New Mexico has a strong spiritual heritage. Not to mention, I'd have the opportunity to get away from the hustle-bustle of my busy job at hospice and be able to take the time to reflect, journal and write. And our earlier plans to visit Chimayo with the sacred dirt and another hot springs site were simply providential. There are no coincidences!

In many ways, it was an overwhelming experience, one that would touch my heart in many ways over the next weeks and months.

It became apparent to me over time that the real healing that occurred during the time in the mineral waters was a spiritual healing. I meditated on the "going forth" message of Jesus many, many times. When Starr placed the angelica oil on my forehead, it exemplified the purpose of my healing – to bring healing to others. I acknowledged my fears and my resistance to telling my story, putting it out there for the world to see, and judge. I had to find the courage and strength to live my life purpose fully. I had to follow Spirit's call, no matter what the consequences would be.

Then we flew off to New Mexico, the first time we'd visited this beautiful state. Our first few days were spent visiting historical sites, with many references to the native peoples and their spiritual beliefs and how the overtaking of their lands by the Spanish led to "conversions" by the Catholic conquerors. It seemed no matter where I turned I was faced with the traditions of native spirituality and Catholic belief. We attended Sunday Mass in the Santa Fe Cathedral and the focus of the sermon was the history of Catholicism in New Mexico – the blending of native spirituality and Christianity. There are no coincidences!

The following morning, we drove north to Chimayo, located in the mountains between Santa Fe and Taos. The small chapel is quite unassuming, and the aged altar is painted in the typical bright colors found in Mexican art. There was a respectful reverence among the few dozen people praying in the chapel. After a brief prayer in the main part of the chapel, we walked to the side room where the pit of the sacred dirt is located. I sat on the concrete floor and placed my feet in the pit. I closed my eyes in prayer, asking Jesus to work through Gary's hands. Gary buried my feet in the dirt, placing his hands over the dirt. Both of us felt the strong healing energies and heat emanating through his hands. We filled two containers with the sacred dirt so that he could continue to spread the dirt over my feet daily during the following months.

As we walked back to the car, there was a horse in the barn yard next to the church. Both of us were struck by this sign, as Spirit Guides can come to us through animals. Spirit Guide horses exemplify the characteristics of strength, grace and beauty – just the words Starr had used a few days earlier at Hot Springs. Gary walked over to the fence, and the horse came over to him immediately. What a beautiful affirmation it was.

Later that day, we spent a few hours at Ojo Caliente, a natural mineral springs water spa. Each pool has a different mineral with different properties and benefits for the physical body. All the minerals felt wonderful on my legs and feet, and Gary's massages were an added treat.

Our vacation ended with a few days in San Diego. We attended Palm Sunday Mass there; Palm Sunday is the beginning of Holy Week. I knew Holy Week this year would hold special significance for me. Before Mass began, I scanned the Gospel readings for the week. I especially pondered Holy Thursday's events, when Jesus had the Last Supper with his Apostles. Before the meal, He washed the Apostles' feet. I have always been moved by this act of humility and faith. The last statement that Jesus makes is this, "Do unto others what I have done for you." Jesus is healing me, so that I can bring healing to others. It is so simple and yet, so profound.

Again I focused on what the effects of my healing will be for others, not just for my own self-centered reasons. Why was this healing occurring in my life now, after all these years? What was I being called to do? I pondered these questions with trust and no fear. I was ready and willing to do whatever I was being called to do. I sat in a place of calm acceptance.

But, most of all, I felt very, very blessed. The events at Hot Springs, Chimayo, and all the small affirmations during this vacation were miraculous. It seemed everything was coming together. I felt the shifts in my being. I no longer viewed myself as the handicapped little girl who grew up to be a physically-deformed woman. My perspective had changed. I now saw myself as a very blessed woman. I had finally awakened to the Healing Spirit and felt the peace and unconditional love of Jesus fully. I was healing spiritually.

I was filled with gratitude and faith and I felt very, very blessed.

Lesson #28: When we believe, we are showered with blessings.

CHAPTER 29

FOLLOWING INTUITION

In Gary's massage center, I have the opportunity to do Reiki sessions for clients, on Saturday's or in the evenings. What I had developed over the past year was a stronger awareness of clients' energy levels. I became more aware of intuitive feelings that I had and learned to trust those intuitions. I started to ask clients if they would like to hear some of the intuitive feelings I experienced, and most clients were open to receiving this information. It seemed everything I shared resonated with them.

I had taken Jesus' words literally – it was time to develop the next level of my healing work. I gained confidence in doing shamanic journeying with others during Starr's workshop. Adding shamanic work to Reiki healing was the next logical step. So, per my usual methodology of gaining knowledge about a topic new to me, I started to read more and more about different shamanic traditions. I was surprised to learn how many traditional cultures have some type of shamanic healing, and how many of these ancient practices are resurfacing in today's modern world. While some traditional practices resonated more with me than other practices, I can honestly say I gained some new perspective from each book.

During Reiki sessions with clients, more things started to occur. I started to see Spirit Guides and angels, and I received clear messages from them for the client. And there were times I even received messages for myself during these sessions! I did not see them visually, in a physical way, but rather I saw them in my imagination, my mind's eye. These spiritual beings appear in clear ways, in form and in color, and speak to me.

One day during a session, I saw an angel actually blend into my body, her hands sending energy through my hands. Another time, I saw several angels placing their hands on various body parts of a client who had pain in several locations. After the treatment, the client told me (before I said anything), she felt many sets of hands on her body throughout the session. She said she had opened her eyes a few times to see where I was standing, as she was trying to figure out where my hands actually were, or if another Reiki practitioner had joined the session!

As the months passed by, all my Reiki sessions included the spiritual element. In other words, various angels and Spirit Guides joined us. I never knew who would show up. I would set the intention for the client to experience healing wherever it was needed, and we would receive the guidance to facilitate that healing. It worked every time.

One day, while perusing a bookstore website, I decided to see what new books on Reiki had been written. And, lo and behold, I found one called "Shamanic Reiki"! Of course, I ordered it immediately. It was very exciting to read this book and realize that other Reiki practitioners were doing a similar type of work – how validating.

The major lesson for me in doing Shamanic Reiki work is simply this – trust, trust, trust. I had listened to my intuitive guidance and blended these two healing modalities together. It had just felt right and natural. I had not questioned it, or doubted that I should be adding this element to my Reiki sessions with clients. I went with the Divine Flow, and both the clients and I were enriched by this blessing.

This is how intuition works – it is a way to live in Divine Flow and be in communication with Spirit. Generally, we are not struck by lightening, moving from a state of non-awareness to total awareness. We are given feelings and thoughts on a daily basis. The problem is most of us dismiss those feelings and thoughts as crazy, or something we just made up – I know this is true, as I did that myself for many years. Through my reading and life experiences, I started to make the decision to trust my intuitive thoughts more frequently. When these thoughts were validated by clients, my confidence and trust levels grew even more, and my intuitive senses became sharper. Then the messages became even clearer and stronger and soon visual experiences became a part of my healing work with clients.

And intuitive work became a part of my own healing process. Both Gary and I developed the ability to understand what was occurring during his healing work with me. One evening, while Gary was doing Reiki on my legs, something unusual happened. My legs started to move, shaking back and forth, and up and down. Both of us were amazed, as these movements continued for fifteen or twenty minutes. It was a sure sign that healing energies were flowing through my body and the healing process was continuing. Gary strongly felt the movements were affirmations that positive vibrations were flowing and healing my legs and feet. The more we listened to our intuition, the more blessings we received. When a person pays attention to spiritual guidance through intuition, many blessings occur.

After that evening, the movements occurred every time Gary did Reiki on my legs. Soon it was happening every time I did Reiki on my legs, usually every morning before getting out of bed and every night before falling asleep.

One quiet Sunday morning, I decided to journey and connect with Spirit World. I lay down on our bedroom carpet, with a pillow under my head. As soon as I entered Spirit World, the African tribal leader met me and walked me through the jungle to the healing table. The tribal members greeted me warmly, and the Medicine Man stepped forward. He gave me instructions on how to reposition myself on my bedroom floor. He asked me to place a pillow under my knees and turn my body, so that my legs were next to the edge of the bed. He wanted my legs to be straight and next to each other – they had been in a relaxed position, slightly apart from each other. He instructed me to take several deep breaths and relax.

My mind returned to the tribal scene, and the Medicine Man led the group in a healing ceremony. While I watched them in the Spirit World, I was aware of my legs shaking in the physical world. The connection between the two worlds became more real to me, as the two realities merged in this journeying experience. My legs continued to shake for about ten to fifteen minutes, until the leader stepped forward and stated it was time to end the session.

The leader then gave me some information. First, he stated that we have started on a new level of healing and more physical healing is fast approaching. He gave me specific instructions for the next few weeks. He asked me to detoxify my body gently, by decreasing the amount of food I eat and eating healthy foods only. He gazed at me with loving eyes, and He revealed Himself to me as Jesus. I expressed gratitude to Him, to the Medicine Man, and to the tribe for the extraordinary experience.

During my journaling after the session, I started to remember the first shamanic healing session, almost two years earlier, when the same African tribal leader gave me specific instructions to choose a shell and to journal my experiences. Jesus has been with me every step of the way, every day of my life.

My heart filled with love for Jesus, as I pondered my lifetime of being connected to Him. Memories flooded back. One of my earliest memories was my First Communion Day when I first received the Communion host. We Catholics believe it is truly the Body of Jesus, not a symbol. How many hundreds of times have I received the Host – and not been truly aware of this miracle? How many times has He spoken messages to me that I have not heard? How many times has He appeared to me, through dreams, visions, other people, and I did not recognize Him?

Through the shamanic healing sessions, He came across as Jesus for the first time, (the human/divine man born in

Bethlehem), prior to our venture to Hot Springs. Now, I realized He was always present, in all the sessions. Usually, He was in the background, acting as the Director of the session, and not showing Himself to us.

The lesson for me is that the Divine Spirit is always with us and we need to learn to see Him in all things – nature, animals, people, Spirits. He chooses to reveal Himself to us in ways that we can understand at that point in our lives. He reveals Himself to us within our own culture and life experience. When I broadened my understanding of how the Spirit World communicates to us, His revelations could occur in more varied ways in my life, as I was open to seeing Spirit in more than one way, the Christian definition.

Then a few weeks later, I received another physical, earthly affirmation. It had been a year since I saw the physical therapist who recommended normal shoes with orthotics, as a replacement to orthopedic shoes. It seemed important to see him again, so I made a follow-up appointment. He greeted me warmly with a big bear hug. I was excited that he even remembered me! He immediately noticed I was walking better, with a less pronounced limp. I sat down on the table and showed him my more muscular feet and legs. He saw how the long surgical scars on the front of each shin had shifted about half an inch, to the inner side of the leg. He stared in total amazement, stating he had never seen results like this in a post-polio patient. I reminded him that I practiced Reiki often and was working with an intuitive shamanic healer, and he nodded knowingly.

He then called another physical therapist into the room to show her these changes. Soon both of them were staring at my legs with their mouths wide open. He used the "miracle" word several times. His explanation of the scars moving is that my legs have actually rotated in the hip joints, enabling them to become straighter.

Although my physical body still bears many effects of polio, real physical changes have occurred. Just the fact that my walk has changed after these many decades seems miraculous. To have the professionals be amazed was a great affirmation!

Lesson #29: Trusting intuition leads to spiritual growth.

CHAPTER 30

BEING CALLED TO SERVICE

Several months later, it seemed to be the time to have another shamanic healing session with Starr. Gary would be away for five days, studying an additional type of massage, called Lomi Lomi. So it seemed it would be the ideal time to schedule an appointment with her. However, Starr had no availability during those five days, and we scheduled the appointment for the following week. While I felt a little disappointed that I had to wait for the session, I also believed everything happens for a reason.

One evening, after a day of training, Gary came home with a message for me, from one of his classmates. This woman told him she had some psychic abilities, but had not developed them, due to being labeled as "strange" in her small Carolina town. The message was that I needed to write. Gary had looked at her in amazement and shared that I had had polio as a child, was experiencing healing, and was in the middle of writing a book about my experiences. She told him this information was an affir-mation to her that she needed to develop her psychic abilities further, and not be fearful. She also asked him if the words, "earth, wind and fire" had any special meaning to him, and he had answered no.

On the fifth day of this training, the same woman presented Gary with several gifts for me, and stated she had been told, during meditation, the words "earth, wind and fire" were actually for his wife, not him. She was guided to select these three items for me. The first was a feather from a hawk, for the wind. The second item was soil from the earth, and the third, ashes from a fire. She instructed Gary to mix the soil and ashes together and place them in a small pouch. The feather was to be attached to the strings of the pouch.

Later that evening, she was guided to give him another gift for me. It was an aqua-colored sarong, with depictions of water and fish on it. Her instructions were for me to take these items to my next shamanic healing session – not knowing that it was scheduled two days later. It became clear to me why I could not meet with Starr, until after Gary's training was over.

So my session with Starr began with a brief explanation of the sarong and gifts. When Starr went to Spirit World, Spirit addressed these gifts immediately. I was instructed to place the sarong across my legs and lay the pouch on my lap, on top of the sarong. I was also instructed to spend meditative time with these items placed across my legs and on my lap, just as they were positioned then. These items could become infused with strong healing energies, assisting in further physical healing for me. We were told these items are to assist me in staying grounded, as it has become so easy for me to travel to the spiritual world and, because it is so peaceful and loving, I would prefer staying there at times!

However, Spirit stated there was an even greater purpose for these items. They were to be used by me while bringing healing to others. I needed to have them in the room with me during Reiki sessions, or other times of healing and teaching. These items would hold the strong healing energies, obtained during times of meditation, and this healing power would be trans-mitted to others to facilitate their healing.

Spirit continued, these gifts were also an affirmation that it was time for my focus to shift. The main focus was Service to Others – bringing healing to others, and expending less time, energy, and focus, on my own healing. My healing has not ended but would continue. I would experience healing, as others were being healed. I no longer needed to focus on further healing for me, as it will occur on its own. Starr also received the message that for the past few years, I had been quite focused on supporting Gary in his new endeavors and had put my intuitive abilities to work with others on the backburner. It was time to claim my own shamanic power, in my own right. He is well on his path, and I needed to find my path.

The session was shorter than usual, but clear and concise. It resonated very strongly with me – I knew the messages were simply Truth. At this point in time, it will be simple to grow into that purpose, as I have been stepping towards it, inch by inch, day by day.

Being called to a life of service – that is really, really exciting to me. It is truly a calling, serving others in a new and more powerful way. No other purpose in life can be more important. As far as my own physical healing is concerned, I realized I really am okay if I have reached the end of the line physically. I am grateful for the improvements that I have experienced, and these are greater than anything I ever imagined as an adult. In the matter of a few years, my physical and emotional health had improved greatly. For the first time in my memory, I am absolutely accepting of what my physical body is. If the rest of my life includes this improved limp, and riding in a wheelchair on day-long sightseeing trips, so be it.

At the same time, Gary was embarking on another new path, by adding Lomi Lomi massage to his repertoire of bodywork. So why did Gary decide to pursue another method of massage therapy? As is typical in our lives these days, it happened quite accidentally – or not. One day, I noticed a new flyer on the bulletin board at Gary's massage space, and we have no idea who placed it there. It advertised the Lomi Lomi training course and gave a brief explanation of this Hawaiian method of massage. I was intrigued by the reference to Lomi Lomi having a connection to Hawaiian spirituality and thought about how it may be similar to his using Reiki during massage, when the client agrees to this additional modality.

When I mentioned it to Gary, his first response was that a five-day training would probably be very expensive and not affordable for us. But I felt strongly it was something he needed to look into and encouraged him to obtain more information, by either visiting the trainer's website, or calling her. When he read more about Lomi Lomi massage online, he also felt attracted to the method. He was greatly surprised to learn the cost of the training, as it was considerably less than either of us anticipated. And then, the biggest sign of all - the training was being held only three miles from our home.

One of the great advantages of being married to a massage therapist is to be the first recipient of his practicing new techniques! A Lomi Lomi massage is very relaxing. There is a flow to it, unlike the typical Swedish massage. Gary learned Lomi Lomi can result in even more emotional releases than other types of massage – and he can also receive messages from the recipient's physical body and from Spirit. His first Lomi Lomi massage for me was simply lovely, and I felt very peaceful.

The following week, I was very excited to experience another one, thinking it would be even more calming, since I knew what to expect. Of course, the unexpected happened. When Gary worked on my right knee, he pressed against it rather hard, and I asked him to please go easy there, as that knee is so vulnerable. Then, a few minutes later, he pressed it again and it felt uncomfortable – I asked him to stop working around that area altogether. I was able to set aside my feelings of irritability during the remainder of the session.

When the treatment ended, however, I felt the need to discuss the "knee incident." Gary mentioned how guarded I am, regarding my legs. I felt defensive and angry. I told him about all the times I had been warned, as a little girl, not to let my legs get hurt, as an injury could be devastating to them. I avoided sports, sometimes due to physical limitations, but even those I could have possibly done, due to the possibility of injury. I had been scared to ride a sled, or ride a horse, or hit a volleyball. Had I put a shield around myself? You betcha. Was I controlling about how my legs could be touched? – yessiree. After a few more minutes of my justifications, and angry comments, the tears started to flow.

I apologized for my outburst and again reiterated how great the massage really was. I felt guilty for not expressing more gratitude to him for the massage. Gary, in his usual calm way, stated this all happened for a reason, as it was obvious I needed to release those fears. Both of us knew his "forgetfulness" to be careful around that knee was a necessary action for these unhealthy emotions to be released. It was obvious to us that deeper levels of emotions were rising to the surface once again. I knew I had just found another emotional area requiring more meditation and journaling. My healing process continues on.

The journaling flowed, as I uncovered another layer of thoughts and emotions. I still held onto an image of my legs being like twigs that could snap with the least amount of pressure. This image was the direct opposite of the one I had been practicing. During a previous session with Starr, I had been instructed to picture my legs as strong and solid as tree trunks. I had visualized that image many times. As a result, I felt more secure standing in a checkout line, or presenting in front of a group at work. The old feelings of insecurity and instability were dissipating. I no longer felt like I would simply topple over, or collapse on the floor.

The knee incident was different though, as I perceived my legs were threatened by possible physical injury. The threat took me back to the old image of twigs, rather than my new tree trunk image. There was an external force that could hurt me, and my physical body could suffer the consequences. This threat, however, was based on old, inaccurate thoughts. Slight pressure on my knees, during a massage, would not break my knees. My bones are strong, with high levels of calcium, and I have no particular joint aches or pains. While my knees are not the knees of a healthy 30-year-old, they also will not break into two pieces, simply from a little pressure. My thoughts did not fit with my physical reality. And the thoughts led to fears, fears that did not match the physical reality.

I was reminded, again, that fear is the opposite emotion of love. Love embraces new experiences, growth and development. Fears hold us back from experiencing the highest potentiality of our beings. We cannot experience the highest realms when we close doors against opportunities presented to us. When we find ourselves saying "no" before we even consider the "yes" possibility, we are living a life based in fear.

My emotion of fear, created by my thoughts of having weak, twiggy knees, created a fear-filled event for me. If I had not explored what this fear was all about, and realize the irrational parts of it, I could have added massage to my list of unsafe activities. This list needs to become shorter, not longer!

My journaling also addressed the question of my healing vs. bringing healing to others. Obviously, my healing is not totally over yet. I realized I will continue to work on changing old thoughts and beliefs during all of this lifetime. Will this emotional healing manifest into more physical healing? I don't know, or care, at this time. What I know is that I trust God more, and the path I am on, and it will work out exactly the way it is supposed to work out. I realized my emotional healing would continue, even as I was focusing on the service aspect of my life. There would be no neat sequence – I would be totally healed – and then I would bring the message of healing to others. Quite the opposite – my continual healing would be part of the lesson for me and, more importantly, be a part of the lesson for those whose lives I would touch. None of us needs to be perfect to live a life of service. In fact, our greatest lessons come from our imperfections, as these bring the deepest insights and understandings.

Once again, I was reminded that the journey of healing is led by wounded healers. As we compassionately share our twists and turns, and ups and downs, others will be touched and encouraged by our struggles. The life of Jesus exemplifies this reality. I always think of His greatest days on earth being those after the Resurrection. He appeared to his disciples and many others, with wounds on His hands, feet and chest. He could have just as easily removed all those reminders of His suffering, but instead He chose to keep them. These visual signs of His suffering and death demonstrate to all of us the wisdom gained through the difficult process of life and death.

This simple thought led to several days of journaling for me – Jesus' life is the perfect example of a life of service.

Lesson #30: We serve others through our own wounded-ness.

CHAPTER 31

MORE ON PROCESS

One day during a meeting at work, I bent my left thumb and noticed a strange, crackling movement in the joint. I repeated it again and again, trying to figure out why it was moving that way. Within a few days, the movement became painful. And another odd thing happened – on the outside of that same thumb, a large red-colored blister appeared. As it turns out, I was scheduled for my annual doctor's visit the following week, so I mentioned these two unusual changes to her.

She stated the odd joint movement is called trigger thumb, and she would make a referral to an orthopedic surgeon for treatment. At the same time, he could consider removing the blister.

During the next few weeks, while waiting for the surgeon's appointment, my left thumb continued to become more painful, and I applied a splint to prevent its movement. I researched the Internet, and it seemed there was no agreement as to what caused trigger thumb – whether it was related to over-use, or if it "just happened." I pulled out my Louise Hays' book and looked up thumb problems, and she notes the psychological issue has to do with holding on to things, hmmmmm…. Having two thumb problems occur at the same time seemed more than just a mere coincidence to me, but I did not explore what the emotional issues around "holding" might be for me.

The surgeon was of the school of thought that trigger thumbs just happen and are not related to any kind of overuse or injury. He gave me a cortisone shot, stating it works about 50 percent of the time. If it did not alleviate the problem, surgery would be the next option. He explained the surgery is minor, requiring two stitches at the base of the thumb. He also wanted to see if the blister would heal on its own. If not, that could be removed at the time of surgery, too. The next appointment was scheduled for three weeks later. Both of us were hopeful the shot would take care of the problem.

It did not. To make the situation even more curious, my right thumb started acting the same way, just a few days prior to the check-up appointment. Since the cortisone shot had not worked and both thumbs were now involved, an outpatient surgical procedure was scheduled for another three weeks later. I knew there had to be something going on with me, on an emotional level.

What was I holding onto? The first thing that came to mind was my old belief system, and how sometimes my thoughts reverted back to viewing myself as a person with physical limitations. Although I had been practicing many healing modalities, it was difficult for me to release that old image of myself. On many levels, I was healing, but the healing was certainly not complete.

One week before the surgery, another problem happened! During the middle of a work day, I noticed a strong sensation in the small of my back. It felt like a muscle was tightening up, and over the next few hours, it became tighter and tighter, and very uncomfortable. By the time I drove home after work, I could barely climb the steps from our garage into our home. I could not wait to find the comfort of our nice, warm waterbed, and I supported my back with layers of pillows. What in the world was going on? It felt like God was trying to give me a message through all these physical manifestations, and I was not getting it!

I called Starr and asked if we could do a session over the phone. Gary was working that evening, and there was no way I could get out of bed and drive to see her. She just happened to be free, and she was more than happy to accommodate my special request. I briefly described my current back problems and the problems with both thumbs. She started by checking in with Spirit and meditated quietly for a few brief minutes. Her first questions were regarding the timeline of when the first trigger thumb occurred, and what else was happening in my life during that time. That was the first time I made the connection to a family health crisis.

One of my younger brothers had experienced a stroke earlier in the fall, and there were still many concerning symptoms. The first trigger thumb occurred about two weeks after the stroke. In fact, my siblings and I had just visited him and his wife a few weeks earlier. While it was a blessed trip in many ways, it was also very difficult to visually witness his fatigue and struggles in dealing with everyday tasks.

Starr stated that when physical problems occur with thumbs, that is often indicative of worrying about the details of life. Spirit told her that I continue to do the "emotional carrying" in my family. As the oldest child, I continue to feel some level of responsibility towards the other eight. I explained to Starr that on the surface, my relationships with my siblings are healthy and appropriate. I am not a "mother figure" in the sense that I call them constantly and give them advice, or am overly-involved with their day-to-day lives. However, I agreed that I have a strong emotional bond, and on a deeper, subconscious level, I do feel responsible, somewhat anxious, and worried about how all of them are doing. Spirit's words certainly resonated with me.

She also was given the message that the newest pain, in my lower back is associated with family, and with power. It was now time to hand over this emotional burden to my siblings. I needed to trust that each of them is on their own path, and everything is proceeding along in their lives, just as it is meant to be. Cognitively, I have that belief but emotionally, I was still carrying the burden of making sure all of them were safe and secure in their lives. I hated to admit that I am still a worrier, although I know worry is based in fear and not in trust.

Through Starr, Spirit gave me some specific instructions regarding several back exercises, and the pain started to decrease significantly that evening and was totally gone within twenty-four hours. The processing work regarding the emotional burdens, however, was just beginning. Spirit had specific instructions for that too. He told Starr I could release the emotional carrying of my siblings, by sending Reiki to them. In fact, sending them love and light was the best gift I could give them. At the same time, Reiki going forth from my hands would be healing for my thumbs. I could also send Reiki to my heart chakra to facilitate the releasing of fears for my siblings.

Holding on, holding on, holding on. Was it just about the special bond I feel with my four brothers and four sisters? I journaled several times on this question to explore all the ways I feel connected to them. Not only did I help care for most of them when they were babies and little children, but my emotional caring for them was accelerated by my Dad's death. Because Mom did not cope well, she left the younger children to their own devices, and I knew their adolescent years included a lot of partying and risky behaviors. I had prayed for all of them, all of the time.

When Gary and I moved away from Indiana after our wedding, my worrying only worsened. It seemed all I could do was try to convince Mom those children needed her guidance and discipline, and I worried about them all the time. Somehow, they all survived those years and created successful lives for themselves, each and every one of them. I always felt my prayers had a part in that. And reconnecting with my Dad and other relatives through mediums had given me more reassurance that many people had been guiding and protecting them.

Then I realized I have done the same thing with my own two adult children. On the surface, we raised them to be very independent and encouraged them to pursue their dreams. I have always been supportive of their career moves and the decisions they've made in their lives. I am very careful about what I say to them, not trying to interfere in their lives, but letting them know I love and support them.

But underneath – well, that's a different story. I am strongly attached to them emotionally. I had to find the right balance between loving them, and not worrying about them. Several nights before falling asleep, I laid with my hands, palm sides up, visualizing emotional bonds between them and me. One night, an image came to me. The emotional bonds looked like black ropes. I made the decision to turn those ropes into rays of love and light, rather than worry. My emotional connections need to be based in love, not worry and fear. I also had to trust their lives were proceeding along, just as they were meant to be. Just like Gary and me, I knew both of them had to make their choices, learn their life lessons, and walk on their life paths. I had to accept, on a deep emotional level, that their lives would have love and joy and successes, and hurts and disappointments. And all of it would be for a good purpose. I knew it cognitively, but I had to accept it fully, on an emotional level.

Another night, I took a journey into Spirit World with the intention of gaining more insight into my always needing to "hold on" to other people. I saw hundreds of black ropes emerging from my palms, and I followed the ropes to hundreds and hundreds of people. I visualized cutting all the black ropes, freeing all these people from an unhealthy emotional bond with me. Instead, I sent all these people love and light, through Reiki. My heart chakra was bursting with love for them, and for all people.

Then, the untethered people started coming back to me, in groups of three or four. I recognized some of the people – there were schoolmates, old friends, coworkers from previous jobs, relatives, clients and patients, people whose names I did not even know. My impression was there were many people that I had helped in some way, such as listening to their worries, or providing professional counseling. There were others to whom I had just given a smile in a store, or said a kind word to them. Each group thanked me for being a part of their lives and then they flew off. They looked like angels, with wings on their backs.

It was a beautiful journey and warmed my heart. It showed me the compassionate care I have given to others in this lifetime, and now it was time for me to be grateful for these many opportunities to show love. But, I needed to release these experiences and let these people get on with their lives! I played my small part, it was appreciated, and it was time for all of us to move on. This was a very powerful experience for me, one that I will never forget.

The day for the trigger thumb surgery finally came, and the surgery itself went very smoothly. And, I thought I was getting a "hand-le" on the many aspects of my emotional self that needed releasing. Both hands were bandaged up with layers of gauze and wrappings – funny how big those bandages were for two small stitches on each hand! I was instructed to take off the bandages four days later and cover the stitches with band-aids. That sounded simple enough.

Instead, it turned into quite a traumatic event. The gauze material had become stuck to the area around the stitches, as a little bleeding must have occurred after the surgery. While my poor husband tried to gently pull the gauze away, I experienced the closest thing to a post-traumatic event I've ever had. Fear overcame me, and I sobbed uncontrollably, my body shook, and I became very cold. I experienced flashbacks to two times in the summer of 1960, the summer I had my leg surgeries.

The most traumatic aspect of the surgeries on my legs and feet were the removal of the stitches. It was very painful as the skin had grown over the stitches – and there were dozens of stiches to remove. The entire area was still very sore and tender from the surgery itself. I went back in time, emotionally, to being the little girl, crying and screaming at the top of her lungs, pleading them to stop hurting me. It hurt so very, very much – I could not stand it. So, this night, almost fifty years later, I reverted back to that emotional state – and, I could not stop the flood of emotions. Eventually, with several long pauses, when Gary guided me to breathe deeply and giving me Reiki to regain some calmness, he was able to pull the gauze off my hands.

Although this was an unpleasant event to live through, I can honestly say those old, painful emotional memories are finally gone. It was time for them to be released. Several more days of Reiki healing and journaling facilitated this necessary emotional work.

Why did I have trigger thumbs? I know, and I mean, I really know, there were a multitude of reasons for these physical manifestations. I was holding on, too tightly, to too many things and people – my old belief system, painful memories, the family members I love, the list goes on. When we hold on too tightly, we cannot trust the process of life. We do not truly trust God, and we do not trust that sometimes people have to go through their own difficult times, to learn their life lessons – this includes my wonderful brothers and sisters, and my precious children and grandchildren.

Another lesson in the process of healing was finally learned by me – healing is a continual, lifelong process. As one layer of our emotional and spiritual selves is healed, a deeper layer rises to the surface for its own healing. My trigger thumbs were a physical manifestation of holding onto people in my life. I thought I had to care for everyone emotionally – the opposite of trusting. The traumatic event of removing the bandages became an opportunity to finally heal the emotional scars resulting from the removal of stitches in 1960. Yes, the healing continues and continues....

Lesson #31: Healing is a continual, lifelong process.

CHAPTER 32

GIFT OF GRACE

It's been a year since our trip to Hot Springs and I felt an urge to visit those amazing mineral waters again. Here we were again – the last week of March, the week leading up to Palm Sunday this year and, in another week, it would be Easter Sunday. It is also the week of my father's birthday. This year, he would have been 82 years old on March 24. It is always so hard to picture him as an elderly man, since he left this earth at the young age of 43 years. I thought of him many times during this week and I felt his presence around me several times.

Gary and I drove up on a Friday evening, after a busy week of work and tasks, to enjoy the waters and relax. We also decided it might become a spiritual journey and were simply open to any possibility. On our hour-long drive, I said a prayer and invited Jesus to join us.

The evening was cool and gray, the perfect weather for resting in the warm waters. We were assigned to one of the hot tubs sitting next to the river. We were greeted by a fully churning river, full of the waters of melting snows after an exceptionally cold winter in western North Carolina. Gary spent most of the time massaging my legs and joints. It seemed more emotions were released from my body; the layers and layers continue to rise within me to be released.

The following morning, I was drawn to a book I had purchased a few years ago, but unfortunately had not spent any time studying. It is called "Healing with Crystals and Chakra Energies," written by Sue and Simon Lilly. Guess what is on the cover? A picture of a beautiful blue rock that looks exactly like the one I purchased a year ago, at the direction of Jesus! In the past year, I used this crystal many times during Reiki and meditation. I had placed the beautiful crystal on our headboard bookshelf, directly above my head while I slept.

I read the section on this rock and the information correlated perfectly with the messages and the journey that I have lived this past year. The crystal is called celestite and let me quote from the book: "Celestite has an uplifting, calming and expansive quality, making it good for contemplation and meditation. It is effective at lifting heavy moods and sadness as well as balancing the throat chakra. The ethereal quality of celestite crystals often helps the mind to travel beyond its normal perspective, promoting inspiration and intuitive leaps." I do not think I could have described this past year more perfectly!

The throat chakra is the communication center of the body, and communication is a two-way street. It is the energy center of receiving messages, and it is the center of transmitting, or teaching, those messages. Many of us have been trained to shut down this center, whenever parents or teachers dismissed our ideas and thoughts as insignificant or inappropriate, or simply wrong. We learned to doubt our own truths and learned not to speak them out loud anymore.

Learning more about a healing tool that I had been using but not fully appreciating gave me, yet again, a new topic on which to meditate and journal. I started to appreciate the many gifts that Divine Source has given to me, and I journaled on the Gift of Grace.

The Gift of Grace is beautiful to contemplate. We can look back on the many events in our lives and identify the times when the Universe has reached out and extended the gift of love and peace to us. Abundant gifts of grace surround us at all times, but often we are not aware of all these gifts.

The Gift of Grace is about being open to, and receiving, all the wonderful gifts from the Divine. And then it is about passing on these same wonderful gifts to other people, animals and all living things in the universe. Every time we receive a compassionate word from another, we are living in Grace. Every time we speak a compassionate word to another, we are living in Grace. Expressions of love, empathy, kindness, and forgiveness are examples of grace, whether we are the recipients or the givers.

My story has now come full circle – it begins with faith and now is being fully expressed through grace. The Gift of Grace is the action component of the Gift of Faith. Faith encompasses our beliefs and our knowings, of the Divine. Grace is the action of accepting Divine gifts and passing them onto others.

When all people strive to live to the best of their abilities, then all of us can participate in the Dance of the Universe. Negative energies, like hatred and jealousy and fear, will disappear. No negative energies at all? Is that even possible? But isn't that what we call heaven? And isn't it possible to create heaven on earth? All of us can remember small glimpses of heaven that we have experienced – holding a newborn baby while he stares straight into your eyes; feeling God's presence in a church or in the woods; finding the Sacred Space through meditation. Grace is that "ahhhhhhh" moment, resting in the unconditional peace and love of God.

Those special, grace-filled moments happen more frequently in my life now. It's not that grace is showing up more often – rather it is that I recognize those moments when they happen.

I love contemplating the many gifts I have received just in the past few years. Somehow, some way, I opened up my heart and soul to say "yes" to the gifts that appeared in my path. Where would my life be, if I had not said "yes" to Reiki? To alternative healers? To Gary changing careers? To God? To the blessings of faith and grace? Where would I be?

Lesson #32: Grace is the experience of the unconditional peace and love from God.

CHAPTER 33

ALL IS CONNECTED

May 11 is my mother's birthday and this year it was a very special day. It was a typical day at work but I thought of Mom often. After all, I became aware of hospice services through her illness and death and now I am working in a hospice agency. I remembered her love of telling stories and I remembered our journey together on earth, both the good times and the difficult times. I felt compassion and love for her. What a difficult life she had, too many deaths of people she loved. I prayed for her healing to continue on the other side.

Our evening at home was not unlike our typical evenings after a day of work and household chores. Gary and I finally sat down together, relaxing and catching up on the day's events. His hands rested on my legs, as he gave me Reiki energy. As usual, my right leg jumped and vibrated every time one of us did Reiki on me, and tonight it started again. But, all of a sudden, there was a huge movement! It was as if Someone lifted up my thigh bone and realigned it in my hip socket. We stared at my leg and at each other in pure amazement. I got up and walked around, somewhat awkwardly. There were mild physical sensations in the area, as if the muscles had to function differently. Would there be another physical improvement?

The following morning, before getting out of bed, I placed my hands on my hip joints to give myself Reiki, like I do many mornings. Yes, the joints on both sides of my hips felt totally different! When I got out of bed, both Gary and I noticed a real but subtle change in my gait – a little straighter, again. For the next few days, I noticed how the muscles needed to operate differently to support this realignment. The improvements continue, slow but sure.

This most recent improvement occurred on my Mother's birthday, and I know in my heart that her intervention was a part of this latest small miracle. My heart filled with gratitude and love for her – and for God, the Divine Spirit who continues to bless me with His gifts. I know that God is with me, and has always been with me, every step of the way.

Question: "Where is God?" Answer: "God is everywhere." I memorized that question and answer many years ago, while learning my earliest Baltimore Catechism lessons in first grade. So simple and yet so profound. So hard to fully grasp.

God is everywhere. We live our lives thinking that we are separate beings, each with our own physical bodies, thoughts, emotions, spirituality: beings unto ourselves. We think that our negative thoughts and our emotions have little or no impact on others, unless we strike out in anger or intentionally hurt someone in some concrete way. We think our positive thoughts and emotions have little impact on others, unless we put them into compassionate action. These beliefs are false, covering up the real truth.

The truth is that God, the Divine Source, the Universe, is everywhere, and our thoughts, emotions and actions do have an effect on the Universal Whole. In other words, everything we do, everything we think, everything we feel, has an effect. Yes, the butterfly flapping its wings causes a ripple effect around the world. We are not separate beings, living in compartmentalized worlds, like silos lined up across a prairie horizon. We are inter-connected to each other in ways that are almost impossible to comprehend. We are connected through our inner worlds and through our external actions. Each of us creates energy through our thoughts, emotions and beliefs, and our energies affect all living things.

So does that mean my story affects you personally? Yes, it does. And does it mean that your story affects me and everyone else personally? Yes, it does. If you treat another person with compassion and love, the ripple effect of the positive, loving, energetic vibration spreads like a loving haze over all the earth. It affects the humans, the animals, plants, minerals, the spiritual realm – everything. Likewise, negative energies develop another kind of haze: the hazes of fear, hate, loneliness, destruction. Each of us has choices to make.

The purpose of my story, of this book, is to start another ripple effect. I am healing myself in my thoughts, my emotions and my physical body. Through this ripple effect, a new wave of healing energetic vibration begins, spreading itself over the earth. It may greatly affect a few, it may subtly affect many. I do not have all the answers. What I know is this – I am a Child of God, with the Divine Source within me and around me. God is everywhere. I made the choice to drop this small pebble of my healing into this magnificent pool of humanity and Divinity – and how far the ripples go… only time will tell, I do not know.

God's unconditional love for all of us is the ultimate healing vibration. Each one of us has access to His love and healing powers.

My story is simply one of a life journey. And, like all life journeys, it has been filled with ups and downs, sorrows and joys. It is an ongoing journey, one that is not yet finished. Over the past few years, I have experienced incredible healing as I discovered that I was never alone. Throughout my entire life, I was, and continue to be, a beloved person. I realized the abundant love and support that always encircled me – from my loving family and friends on earth, my healers, my ancestors and Divine Spirit.

My physical body has changed – my legs are stronger and straighter; my limp is less pronounced. And, I love buying new shoes! More importantly though, I have come to realize that my broken body was only broken in my own mind. In the same way, it is now whole, in my own mind. Not only have I accepted the affliction of my childhood, I have actually grown to embrace it and bless it. I know that I chose the experience of polio, and all its after-effects, to learn the lessons I needed to learn during this lifetime – and the lessons I needed to teach others, whose paths I've crossed, during this lifetime. The experience of polio and all the experiences of my life are truly blessings! My soul overflows with genuine gratitude.

Polio led me down a path of imagined separateness from others for a number of years. Like so many other people, who think they are different in some way from others, a sense of wounded-ness is formed. This illusion can be healed.

Healing is available to each and every one of us. If we are open to healing, the Universe will present the right person, the right method, the right next step, to us – and then we make the choice whether to say "yes" or "no" to that wonderful possibility. Healing comes from within our Divine souls. But often, we need that person or method to rediscover the Healing Source within ourselves. In my life, I've had many healers – from my loving husband, to Reiki practitioners, to psychics, to shamanic healers. Along with those blessings were my traditional Christian beliefs, and my foundation of faith and prayer.

I've come full circle. Think about it – Jesus showing up at my shamanic healing sessions! Why should that sound so crazy? Is that any crazier than His Presence is real, in a small host? Both are real to me. After all, Jesus is the Divine Master of love and healing and His ministry included many physical healings. So often, our spiritual healings begin with physical ones. Jesus continues to want to heal us, but how many of us are open to this possibility? Does it make sense that His healings stopped when He left this earth? No, it does not. Jesus, or Whoever represents your Divine Source, is alive and available to each person on earth. We simply have to "believe and it is true."

The very best part of my story is this: I am not done yet!! My life journey continues, and I truly believe I have more healings coming – on the physical, emotional and spiritual levels. I am dancing right now – at least on the emotional and spiritual levels – and who knows? Maybe some day I will be dancing gracefully on this earth in this lifetime....

Lesson #33: Divine Spirit – God - is everywhere and connects everything.

4222

LIFE LESSONS

Lesson #1: Everyone has a story, full of learning opportunities.

Lesson #2: Faith in God is a true blessing.

Lesson #3: We create our reality through our thoughts.

Lesson #4: When we say "yes" to God-given opportunities, wonderful things happen.

Lesson #5: The Universe graces us with many gifts, when we are open to receiving them.

Lesson #6: Our loved ones, in spirit, continue to love and support us.

Lesson #7: Healing is always a possibility in our lives.

Lesson #8: We can learn how to connect to Spirit.

Lesson #9: Synchronicities are God's way of getting our attention.

Lesson #10: We can create purposeful, loving lives through intention.

Lesson #11: We attract positive – and negative – energies into our lives.

Lesson #12: Saying "yes" to new opportunities enriches our lives.

Lesson #13: We must be responsible, active participants to create purposeful lives.

Lesson #14: We choose to live in abundance, or lack.

Lesson #15: We can choose to live in rhythm with the Universe.

Lesson #16: God graces us with affirmations when we live in alignment with Spirit.

Lesson #17: Spiritual growth creates integrated wholeness.

Lesson #18: True healing begins with me.

Lesson #19: Balance is essential in creating wholeness.

Lesson #20: We can choose to work with the Spirit World in many different ways.

Lesson #21: We receive many blessings when we live our life purpose.

Lesson #22: We live in a world of unlimited possibilities.

Lesson #23: Life is full of many learning and healing opportunities.

Lesson #24: We are spiritual beings, living in physical bodies.

Lesson #25: God places the right people in our lives at the right time.

Lesson #26: True healing occurs in mind, body and spirit.

Lesson #27: Living in Divine Flow is living fully in the physical world and living fully with Spirit.

Lesson #28: When we believe, we are showered with blessings.

Lesson #29: Trusting intuition leads to spiritual growth.

Lesson #30: We serve others through our own wounded-ness.

Lesson #31: Healing is a continual, lifelong process.

Lesson #32: Grace is the experience of the unconditional peace and love from God.

Lesson #33: Divine Spirit – God - is everywhere and connects every-thing.

RECOMMENDED READING

The Power of Flow: Practical Ways to Transform Your Life with Meaningful Coincidence, by Charlene Belitz and Meg Lundstrom, published by Three Rivers Press.

Trust Your Vibes: Secret Tools for Six-Sensory Living, by Sonia Choquette, published by Hay House.

A Little Light on Spiritual Laws, by Diana Cooper, published by Hodder and Stoughton Ltd.

Crossing Over, by John Edward, published by Princess Books.

After Life, by John Edward, published by Princess Books.

Animal Spirit Guides, by Stephen D. Farmer, PhD., published by Hay House.

You Can Heal Your Life, by Louise L. Hay, published by Hay House.

Abundance Through Reiki, by Paula Horan, published by Lotus Press.

Empowerment Through Reiki: The Path to Personal and Global Transformation, by Paula Horan, published by Lotus Press.

Synchronicity & You: Understanding the Role of Meaningful Coincidence in Your Life, by Frank Joseph, published by Element Books.

Healing with Crystals & Chakra Energies, by Sue and Simon Lilly, published by Barnes & Noble Books.

Journey of Souls, by Michael Newton, published by Llewellyn Publications.

Destiny of Souls, by Michael Newton, published by Llewellyn Publications.

Embracing the Tie That Bind: Connecting with Spirit, by Carole J. Obley, published by Xlibris Corporation.

I'm Still With You: True Stories of Healing Grief through Spirit Communication, by Carole J. Obley, published by O-Books.

The World is as You Dream It: Teachings from the Amazon and

Andes, by John Perkins, published by Destiny Books.

Shamanic Reiki: Expanded Ways of Working with Universal Life Force Energy, by Llyn Roberts and Robert Levy, published by O Books.

Shaman, Healer, Sage, by Alberto Villoldo, published by Harmony.

Traveling between the Worlds: Conversations with Contemporary Shamans, by Hillary S. Webb, published by Hampton Road Publishing Company.

About the Author

Deborah is a Usui and Karuna Reiki Master, incorporating shamanic intuitive techniques into her Reiki sessions. Additionally, she is a certified holistic therapy practitioner. She provides trainings for all levels of Reiki to healing practitioners and conducts workshops in holistic therapy modalities. Her belief is that all healing practitioners must manifest their own journeys of healing to be authentic, effective healers and teachers. She is a licensed clinical social worker and works with a hospice agency in Asheville, North Carolina. Her loving, compassionate spirit emanates her first book, and she happily anticipates meeting like-minded folks during future speaking engagements.

BOOKS

O is a symbol of the world, of oneness and unity. In different cultures it also means the "eye," symbolizing knowledge and insight. We aim to publish books that are accessible, constructive and that challenge accepted opinion, both that of academia and the "moral majority."

Our books are available in all good English language bookstores worldwide. If you don't see the book on the shelves ask the bookstore to order it for you, quoting the ISBN number and title. Alternatively you can order online (all major online retail sites carry our titles) or contact the distributor in the relevant country, listed on the copyright page.

See our website **www.o-books.net** for a full list of over 500 titles, growing by 100 a year.

And tune in to myspiritradio.com for our book review radio show, hosted by June-Elleni Laine, where you can listen to the authors discussing their books.

MySpiritRadio